C000271224

# SOUL
# SURVIVOR

# SOUL SURVIVOR

## HOW AN ABANDONED CHILD WENT FROM
## NOTHING TO EVERYTHING

## ROBERT IAN BONNICK

# CONTENTS

## Acknowledgements

A massive thank you to my family, Marina and our two kids Alexa and Almira, for putting up with me being antisocial at times, and forever supporting me! I wrote most of this book on my mobile phone whilst sitting in the passenger seat of our minibus sightseeing in Bali. Thank you to New Holland Publishing, especially Monique Butterworth and Fiona Schultz for showing faith in me – this is my first book! Very special thanks to both Robbie Rommers for the cover shot and Mark Carter for inviting me to crash his photo shoot in the first place! Thank you to my long-time surrogate mum of sorts, Judi Hausmann, for advising reading and assisting me in this endeavour along with giving me invaluable advice over years. Zamba too, for we had over twenty incredible years in business together. A very personal thank you to Gail Franklin and Monty Edwards from 3 The Ridgeway itself for helping to collate all the information, including the acquisition of my confidential file. Finally, probably the most important thank you, to all the kids, members of staff, cleaners and my Chingford friends who gave me all the experiences and taught me all that I hold dear now – for there would be no book without you!

## A special message from
## Robert Ian Bonnick

**M**y life is a testament to 'it's not where you are from, but where you are going' that is important. I grew up in two children's homes in London enduring, racism, classism, a stutter, a lisp, being bullied emotionally and physically and ridiculed. Yet I have managed to achieve so much that wasn't in my life's trajectory back then! Most of my fellow orphans failed to live up to their potential and ended up dropping out of school, in jail, or worse... dead. Whereas I lived, finished higher education, travelled the world, represented my country at the highest level in sport, was a key participant in a business voted number three in the world, have functional relationships, found my soulmate and sired a family. Most where I grew up gave up, whereas I never stopped hustling, pushing expanding and looking to embrace more of life. Most had a negative view on a world that was rarely kind to them, whereas as I nurtured a positive attitude, saw the best in people and studied with some of the most enlightened self-development gurus and meditation masters on the planet to get my attitude right. Most believed they weren't worthy of fulfilling their dreams; I ended up working with supermodels such as Naomi Campbell and legends like Madonna, to name a few.

Please understand that I'm not bragging. If you knew me – and you will do if you decide to read on – you would realise that I'm almost the opposite. I am an introverted extrovert, with a keen sense of duty to help uplift people, be they strangers or friends, often putting their desires ahead of my own, a person who is driven especially to support at-risk youth, as it reminds me of how I grew up. I am a person who doesn't take myself seriously, a bit of a larrikin who is as flawed and fallible as the next person. But the message of hope, inspiration and fulfilment I do take seriously.

Through all these experiences I tripped over five keys which, when executed properly, would bring me the opportunities to satisfy my heart's desires. I realised that if I could do it from my background then anyone could. This is the reason why I have written this book: to share the central theme that how or where you were brought up doesn't have to determine where you end up in life...YOU CAN! I pass this on, not from a preachy, listen to me as I know everything perspective, rather, as a story of what happened to me each time I used, these five keys and why I strongly believe it will work for you too. I have taken hundreds of people through them, many of whom have achieved breakthrough results. They also form the backbone of my keynote address aimed at the youth market.

The first part of this book is about my family history, the second and third a journey, which paints the picture of how I grew up in the second children's home from around eighteen months to almost eighteen years of age. The fourth part of the book details how I managed to achieve so much

– whether by total luck, accident or coincidence – when I used the five keys. The fifth part of the book explains the five keys in detail, giving you an opportunity to try and test them out for yourself.

This is an illustration of how I came to discover the five keys, which when applied gave me a measurable, consistent and successful result every time. I highlight successes, achievements and epic failures. This book is a journey of discovery, with some colourful examples from my past to illustrate how I applied each of the keys.

It is my heartfelt wish that you get something out of this journey that propels you to a breakthrough in an important area or areas in your life. Failing that, feel free to have a good laugh at my expense…

# PART I
# BACKGROUND

# CHAPTER 1

# MY FAMILY HISTORY

## My Jamaican family history

My uncle, Ronald A Bonnick, is a nephew of David Bonnick and Beatrice Whyte and thus our history is somewhat intertwined. They were from the district of Beacon, located on the picturesque plateau overlooking the Great Pedro Bluff and the small resort area known as Treasure Beach, in the Parish of St Elizabeth, Jamaica, West Indies. Thus his ancestral lineage is to the famous Barrett family and the Ashanti tribe of Ghana. On his grandfather's side he is the great-great-grand nephew of Ellen Barrett, a cousin of Elizabeth Barrett-Browning, and on his great aunt's side a descendant of the only female national hero of Jamaica, whose name is Nanny of the Maroons. Her two brothers, Charles Cudjoe (Kojo) and Accompong, defeated the British Army several times and a state within a state was born in St Elizabeth named Accompong, to appease the Maroons.

Many people don't realise the significance of this. The Jamaican Maroons were fierce and the British hadn't really lost a battle or endured a loss of face such as this before.

Jamaica's population was formed through two sources, the indigenous population known as the Arawak Indians, who had a South American root; the other, as most know, came as slaves from Africa. In some cases the British in West Africa, perhaps not realising the depth of their folly, put the wise or holy men of the tribe on the same ship as some of the warriors. By the time they reached Jamaica all, or a significant number, of the crew had been brutally murdered and the ship was 'scuttled' and passengers swam ashore and set up a life for themselves in the more remote parts of Jamaica. These were areas of Jamaica not easily accessed due to the dense jungle-like vegetation that encircled it. In this situation, conventional methods of fighting brought no reward, meanwhile the brutal guerrilla tactics employed by the Jamaican Maroons proved extremely effective. Hence the reason why the British signed the first Maroon Treaty, presumably rather than risk losing too much by way of men and resources.

You need to understand what Jamaicans are like. On one side, the 'Cool Runnings' stereotype – and yes Jamaicans are that very friendly, jovial, considerate and outgoing, but that's not telling the whole story. I already mentioned the Jamaican Maroon stock from where part of me came; fierce warriors, who took the British Army to task on more than a few occasions – and they weren't minor skirmishes! They underpinned much of the American Civil Rights Movement including Marcus Garvey and Malcolm X as well as Colin Powell. In London, for a time, the 'Yardies' were known as one of the most fierce, extremely cold-blooded and violent groups. Now that's the men! Some of the Jamaican women, according to those who know, have been and are even more formidable!

# CHAPTER 2

# MUM AND DAD

I wish I had a chance to hear Mum's side of the story too, but this story comes from Dad and I've no reason not to take him at his word. Both my parents, Josalin and Lambert, came from Jamaica. My mother from Saint Elizabeth and my father from the Parish of St Catherine. Back in the 1950s and '60s many West Indians were attracted to migrate to the UK; let's just say propaganda may have had a little to do with it! They were convinced that the streets of London were paved with gold and you could earn and return rich! The 'streets' part was true, as many ended up performing menial tasks that the Anglo Saxon custodians neither wanted nor had the stomach to do. Thus many West Indians were marooned in London without enough money to return. Both my parents would have found themselves in a very difficult situation. On my father's side he lived in the halfway house of a distant relative. It wasn't unknown for these types of places to sleep ten to a room. My dad worked his behind off and ultimately found himself the trade of electrician, and many years later would own his own home.

This is another thing about Jamaicans, they are industrious people, most of whom value education high and above most other facets of life, and in but a few generations occupied such lofty positions as barristers, lawyers, doctors and the like. But that's another story...

When my mother came to London she stayed in the house of relatives in East London and once again I knew that her life was extremely difficult. It is unfortunate that I know so little of my mother's origins apart from this, which is a real shame!

London at this time had an underbelly of strife, racism, rioting and social unrest to pick a few. The life of a Jamaican immigrant was very tough (to say the least). Also, being so far from home, it's no wonder that many sought refuge with their own kind where there was some sense of familiarity.

So my dad Lambert and my mum Josalin met and had my elder sister, Carol and I quite quickly. Mum already had a son from another relationship, my half-brother Carlton. My memories of Carlton are of a tall, strong-looking man with a bad temper and prominent body odour from a time he came to play ping pong at the children's home. I was born in Homerton Hospital in Hackney on 13 October 1969. I would describe my parents' relationship as a fatal attraction of sorts. My dad told me that the last time he saw my mother she had threatened him violently, letting him know in no uncertain terms what would happen if he left her.

With two children and without any parents or support

around to share the load, I have an insight into what couples go through; the hardships, the non-stop nature of giving giving giving to your young ones, feeding, nappy changing, sleep deprivation; it is relentless, and that's without postnatal depression. Add to this being in a foreign land struggling to make ends meet and the fact that later on my mum was diagnosed with schizophrenia and these are some of the main reasons why I hold nothing against my parents.

However, one day I guess things just got too much! We were left at the doorstep of the halfway house where my father was staying with a change of nappies and food. According to the records our mum deserted us at the address where my father was staying. It was 1 am on Sunday 21 February 1971. I was one and a half years of age and was in a cot with my sister standing beside me.

When my father got home after work, the man in charge told him what had happened. I'm guessing he was a bit overwhelmed! He went to the police station and explained what had happened and that he wasn't in a position to care for us. In the interim, a social worker went to see our mother, who refused to have us back. Apparently she was living in three very small rooms and the conditions were very bad and too difficult for our Mum to cope there with us.

On 25 February 1971 my sister and I were received into care at 287 Kingsland Road, South London, Elephant and Castle. However, we were plucked out of there in a relatively short period of time as my dad felt that there was some kind of abuse going on, and the London Borough Of Hackney placed us into care at 3 The Ridgeway in Chingford.

# PART 2

# HOW I CAME TO DISCOVER THE FIVE KEYS

# WHERE I GREW UP – CHINGFORD

Chingford, years prior to our moving there, was part of Essex. The beautiful Epping Forest was on our doorstep and North Chingford was leafy, green and very wealthy. Chingford had a name: it was the birthplace of the designer of the iPhone, Sir Jonathan Ive , famous footballers, David Beckham and Harry Kane grew up there, music powerhouses East 17 were born just down the road, and the local member was Norman Tebbit, a Conservative MP from the same party as the 'Iron Lady' herself, Prime Minister Margaret Thatcher. North Chingford was very Conservative...

Still, there were some very friendly people in that area too, including the owners of our local corner shop, from whom we received the occasional discount and other random acts of kindness such as free lollies and other items.

South Chingford was, in places, almost the polar opposite of North Chingford. Urban, slightly overpopulated with terrace houses and for all intents and purposes an urban jungle. The epitome of this was the council estate called

Chingford Hall Estate, featuring three very tall concrete skyscraper tower blocks and a subterranean car park linking all three, which would have made a great location to shoot some of the scenes for the second *Terminator* or *Alien* movies. Even during the day it was dark, threatening and somewhat scary, a place you wouldn't walk through, let alone park your car – a place with a bad reputation! I learnt for myself many years later that the description just given was somewhat unfair, when the council provided my sister and I with a flat there on the top floor of St Albans Tower for two years. We never had any issues and were fairly treated by everyone, we even walked home through the car park at night.

# CHAPTER 4

# 3 THE RIDGEWAY CHILDREN'S HOME

The children's home was located at number 3 The Ridgeway, North Chingford, London E4 6RQ and was a large, three-storey Victorian building run by the London Borough of Hackney. It deserved more of a front yard than the one it was blessed with, which was concreted over, but one could argue the backyard more than made up for it; grassy, deep and fairly wide at its best. On the weekends it would double as a football pitch where the two joint swings at the end would be swept to each side, leaving the perfect dimensions for a soccer goal! The local police station was situated less than 100 metres away, almost as a constant reminder of the fact that we were not wanted!

At the age of just under two I entered this place with my elder sister Carol Marlene Bonnick, and it was to be home for more than fifteen years. I recently took receipt of my confidential file, religiously kept for my entire time in the care of The London Borough Of Hackney. The entry below is transcribed for your ease of reading here:

Coming to be received at the Ridgeway, Robert is

not quite as stable as Carol but is working towards becoming so. He still sucks both fingers, which is a source of annoyment to some of the teenage children – especially when they are watching television, as Robert's sucking tends to be noisy. He is sometimes victimised and teased probably because he is youngest and not capable of retaliating verbally or physically. However the staff are aware of this and keep a watchful eye out for any sort of reprisals and unfair attacks upon him. He needs a lot of physical closeness. He has a lot of catching up to do on the lack of mothering earlier in his life. He stills needs to be a baby which he is allowed to be. He is a good footballer and is a member of a local league team. Mother visits every so often; grandma more regularly.'

As I mentioned we had a large front yard that was pathed over, as it really doubled as a car park. Coming in through the front door you were greeted by a large mirror mounted onto the wall. If you turned right, 5 metres directly ahead were the stairs. Prior to reaching the stairs on the right-hand side was the door to the living and TV room. Inside, we had three large bay windows looking out to the concrete front garden.

Back to walking through the front door again, if you turned left in front of the stairs there were two doors. The nearest door took you to the large kitchen which had a central square table with cupboards and cooking appliances all around. If you kept going you reached the back area, which housed the boiler room that powered the house, sinks for laundry, washing machine (which I think was the site of 'the slipper' punishment) then another smaller door out back to the boot room and eventually the back yard. Back to the beginning, by taking the next door, you arrived at our large dining room area, which opened out via the crumbling French doors to our large backyard.

The backyard was split into two. As you opened the doors onto the concrete rectangular play area in front of you, to the left was the wall of the building; here I would spend many hours alone upsetting people with basketball, football or volleying practice (tennis) against it. To the right was the 4-metre-high wooden fence of next door. Straight ahead some 4–5 metres or so was a metre high brick wall and on the other side of it green grass, which went on for 50 metres or more to the end and was 8–10 metres wide. Back to the dining room, which was large enough to double as the games room, where we would set up the table tennis table (full size) and later the almost full-size snooker table too! There was a hatch or a 'pass' connecting the kitchen to the dining room.

To reach the first floor you had to negotiate two sets of very wide, deep, carpeted stairs that switched backed on each other, with each set being around fifteen to twenty steps. You would then arrive at the landing, and a small door to the right opened to the airing room. A large grid structure fabricated in wood housed five storeys of sheets, blankets, pillowcases and bedding of all types. At the top there were wooden ventilation ducts, behind which was the girls' room.

At the landing, between the two large pains of reinforced safety glass, you opened the landing glass door. You would be greeted by a very long, narrow corridor extending from left to right. To the left the large boys' room had a mix of bunk beds and regular beds. Straight ahead to the left after opening the door you'd find five or six tall but fairly narrow windows, side by side. These windows looked down onto the front garden and main road, The Ridgeway, outside. If you peered through some trees you could also see the Police Station diagonally opposite around 100 metres away. This room housed up to twelve or more boys.

Coming back to the landing door, dead ahead there was one medium-sized double room with its own sink and balcony, looking down onto the front of the house. Moving to the right heading down the corridor to the end, the small room on the left-hand side was my sister's room for as long as I can remember, and opposite it was the girls' room. The girls' room perhaps had one bunk bed and the rest were normal single beds. Up to ten or so girls lived in this room. The room had two sash windows that peered out onto the backyard below, where you could clearly see the swings, grass, apple tree, very tall horse chestnut tree and garden shed right at the end beneath it.

The only rooms left in this corridor were two identical bathrooms with toilet, shower and a bath in each. These were side by side on the left-hand side. Lastly, we had Ivan's room right at the end, arguably, the best bedroom in the house and reserved for the oldest or the strongest – and he was both! This large double room was blessed with a balcony that backed onto our backyard below, and due to its elevated position included a view that encompassed all of the glorious surrounding rear gardens that this part of North Chingford had to offer. The room had its own fire exit to the rear garden, so you didn't even have to use the front door anymore either; you could come and go, undetected, as you pleased!

Back to our tour. From the landing you needed to go up one more floor. Once again another two sets of stairs took you there. Once you got up there (the air somehow felt thinner) you had three doors. Straight ahead there was a kind of attic apartment, a very large, self-contained double room. The view was something to behold. It had the same outlook as the kitchen but due to being far higher your vista looked towards Epping Forest and the rest of North Chingford. It also had a trapdoor that came out on the floor below, not far from the door of the girls' room.

The other door to the right was another self-contained attic-type room, a little less glamorous than the one I just described. Nonetheless, it was a great double room with views of the rear garden and that side of North Chingford, and a similar view was shared by the girls' room downstairs.

The final door opened into the smallest of the three rooms, which nonetheless was still large for an office!

Filing cabinets, cupboards…it was mission control for 3 The Ridgeway and held all of the confidential file reviews, notes of important meetings and conversations of a more serious nature in regards to school reviews, social worker reports and personal reports. Up there you felt like you were in your own wing or turret, looking down onto the front garden, The Ridgeway in all its glory, and the police station off in the near distance!

But back to our backyard, I remember the weekends (Sundays I think) twenty or so people playing knockout, which seemed futile for years! There would be one goalkeeper and up to fifteen people trying to score a goal to progress to the next round. I use the word futile, as I was one of the fools trying to skilfully make my way through up to fourteen sets of legs and beat the goalkeeper at the other end! The smart ones would wait close to the goal for the inevitable shot saved by the keeper or a lucky ricochet, tap the ball in and progress to the next round! For many years I was not one of those smart people! In many ways this summed up my time at 3 The Ridgeway, ultimately feeling part of a big, mostly happy family on one hand, and on the other it was about survival and taking advantage of other people's weaknesses to reach your goal! However, sometimes I would ask one of the older ones for help. If they were feeling guilty, unusually sympathetic or generous, they would give it to me – but there was a cost. Recently I bumped into one of the older guys, I won't mention his name, he was laughing (as I was) at how little he paid me when I used to get up at the crack of dawn to help him on the paper round, 'Well you seemed very enthusiastic and didn't complain about the little I was paying you, so I didn't bother changing it!'

That was part of my lot for all of my years I was there; I was the youngest, 'the baby'. I remember, especially in the early years, spending time sucking my two fingers shyly in the corner or cuddling up to one of the members of staff that I felt particularly close to.

There were a maximum of around eighteen kids at any one point in time, the majority of whom were black or coloured. It was a long-stay children's home, not a foster home, nor boarding school, nor boarding house. I was probably there for the longest, as most arrived when they were a little older. However, there were also some tough cases, kids who couldn't really become part of our family and came and went in a matter of weeks or months. Some were too-cool-for-school and thought they knew it all. They had probably been passed around that many children's homes or had such a disturbed childhood that they couldn't acclimatise. Lee, even though he was there for longer, would fall into this category, but more about him later.

Members of staff would take the role of surrogate parents and they, much like us, came in all shapes and sizes, ethnicities, socioeconomic groups, world views and viewpoints on parenting. Some already had children of their own, some didn't, which was very evident. Some, like

Monty Edwards, were West Indian and wanted dearly for the West Indian kids amongst us to know more about our background, culture, food even how to best deal with afro hair! Years later I realised he, unfortunately, met with a great deal of resistance from within. We had student members of staff fresh out of college – imagine that! We had a member of staff cheating on his wife with a work colleague. We had members of staff who believed in corrective measures such as the slipper or the shoe for misbehaving, or washing your mouth out with soap and water if you were foul mouthed – heaven help you if you wet the bed – and the list went on.

The early supervisor of the home I don't really remember but, I was told later by Monty, when Gail took over, things changed for the better under her tenure, which really ended up being the majority of my stay there. An ardent Christian and someone who I believe to this day wanted the very best for us, she genuinely cared for our welfare but probably had her hands tied behind her back by The London Borough of Hackney, in the proverbial sense, on some key methodologies for treating us.

At the time the foster system ran in tandem with the long-stay children's home, each one having its own time in the sun whilst the other was shunned or disapproved of. For whatever reason, when my sister and I came through, long-stay was our selected option, perhaps due to the fact there were two of us, and we would be more difficult to be adopted or fostered than just one child. I also think that the powers that be wanted us to stay together. Only a year or so later my younger, full-blood brother Paul was fostered or adopted to a Welsh professor and their family in Rhydefelen within Aberystwyth in Wales. Robinson was our mother's maiden name which Paul took, whilst Bonnick belonged to our father. By the way, I have to say, growing up with an East London accent and coming across my brother on a trip to Wales to meet him was weird. A tall, immaculately dressed black man with a Welsh accent. Paul was to become a highly regarded hotel manager in London and in Scotland, holding various positions, such as General Manager of The Wolseley and Director of Food and Beverage of the Beaumont Hotel and Colony Grill, both in London. I'm so proud of him and my sister. How interesting that all full-blood siblings ended up in the hospitality industry as my sister Carol has been looking after the VIPs at Stringfellows Nightspot for many years now.

We had a number of 'social workers' over the years assigned to our (myself and my sister's) case but the overarching aim remained the same: to look after our general wellbeing and ensure contact was maintained between ourselves and the rest of our family. I loved, my grandmother (the matriarch of our family) on my mum's side. Then there was my older half-brother Carlton, a tall, well-built man with a bad temper and competitive disposition – at least as far as table tennis was concerned! I had two younger half sisters, Yvonne and Cheryl, who I saw often during my teens, as we competed in the same sporting competitions (different age groups). They seemed lovely but we lost contact after our dear grandmother died. My father had another two boys who were just a little younger than myself and my sister. Rodney is a librarian and Rohan works in the fashion industry. Our social worker didn't know about these last two – I only met them around ten years ago, just after being reunited with my father again, when I was in my mid-thirties.

# CHAPTER 5

# AUNTIES, UNCLES AND THE CLEANERS!

As mentioned previously, members of staff would be entrusted to take the role of surrogate parents. Gail and Monty Edwards I have mentioned already. There were many more than I can remember. Those below, for some reason unbeknownst to me, stayed in my mind.

## Miss Floyd

Miss Floyd was the social worker I probably owe more to than what I can remember, as having recently acquired my confidential file, which was kept on me for the entire time I was at The Ridgeway (and Barnardo's prior), her name is everywhere. All of the meetings and the reviews I had, the important moments of deciding not to be fostered, to dealing with chiropody challenges, meetings with my mum, dad and siblings, her name kept coming forward. It brought the memory of a kind but strong-looking lady with blonde/silver hair and a keen set of eyes (bespectacled too). Wherever you are Miss Floyd, I just wanted to say thank you.

## Auntie Lil

Lillian was from Basingstoke. She was also there for a long time and seems to be another one who gave her life to do her best for all of us kids, from putting us to bed, reading us nursery rhymes, storytelling, going for walks, cooking, cleaning, and I have probably missed out a lot more.

## Eugene

She was another staff member of colour, this time from Barbados. She also had her own family and tried to also teach us about our own blackness, from food, culture perspective and so much more. I loved her cooking and miss her meals to this day – rarely did she seem flustered Eugene. A miracle considering what eighteen kids could try and put you through…every shift!

## Auntie Lesley

Lesley came fairly early on in the piece. If Lil was there the longest (for a member of staff), Lesley would probably be third in line. She was an attractive, caring person who also had the ability to be very strong, forceful, and persuasive when she wanted to be. Being fairly senior in rank within the confines of 3 The Ridgeway, I also got the sense she was a human being with a flaw (as most of us have by nature), and the nature of this work uncovered that. She did her very best to look after and take care of us kids but she found herself in a position which would affect us all in a way I struggle to call positive, but it also revealed life as it truly was. She still remains one of my favourite members of staff over my time there.

## Linda and Tony

Though they came at different times, and unrelated from memory, it seems just to put them together. They were both student trainee staff members, probably finalising part of their social work course with a practical secondment.

Both were very lovely people. Linda came off more as a hippie and Tony, with his handlebar moustache, came across as a more technically minded man, efficient sharp and well schooled. How long they were there for I can't tell you precisely but I remember them fondly.

## Uncle Geoff

He was a proud married black man with a gorgeous family and kids who came to the children's home often. He was also handsome, well studied and well read too. He came to 3 The Ridgeway in the second half of my time there. He had a sharp mind and was for the most part disciplined, timely and on top of his life. But he also, like most of us, had a weakness, one of which would eventually leave us kids in a mixture of awe and sadness…but that's a story for another time. I appreciated Geoff as he was a black role model in a time and place that was in need of one.

## Kate and Steve

Really it should be just Kate (Steve was her husband) but they were inextricably linked for me. Kate had a white, roundish, fresh-faced complexion. She was always positive, incredibly communicative, had a can-do attitude and didn't take herself seriously yet was still a force of nature! I'm pretty sure I just loved Kate straight away! I have some great memories of cutting up potatoes into chips and frying them up before devouring them. Still to this day it blows me away that this is how chips are created! She used to offer practical, emotional advice and wouldn't fail to speak her truth even when it didn't quite go hand in hand with 'the company' line! If there was ever an answer that she didn't have, her husband Steve would. Steve was the polar opposite of Kate in some ways. He was skinny with a darker complexion (perhaps a percentage of Indian extraction in there somewhere) bespectacled, humble, quiet, kind and well meaning. Though he didn't work at 3 The Ridgeway, I remember he always had tools in his car too, therefore perhaps a business in the trades. Together they also made a fantastic couple who balanced each other. Kate, unfortunately, was one of the last members of staff to arrive in my time at 3 The Ridgeway, arriving in the last five years or so of my time there.

### Doris Dowling and Betty Burke

Never underestimate the support the cleaners can give in various stages of your life!

Doris had a family of her own and a son called Nick. I remember from when I was very young, for what felt like the longest time these two women took me in as their own – I know that I owe them a huge debt of gratitude. Whilst the members of staff were given instructions of what they could and couldn't do, there were no such rules when it came down to the cleaners. I remember many times over the years spending time in their company in their home

– fortunately Doris only lived around the corner! They tendered advice, gave critiques of the level of care being given from some of the staff members they didn't approve of – usually where they didn't have much knowledge of how to raise kids themselves.

Doris and Betty had a great deal of empathy for me and my sister. They saw all types of kids institutionalised: those who didn't last; those who just seemed like bad eggs from the start; those who were bullying the others, and so on. They seemed to see everything, including the scandals like the two members of staff – one married with kids – who would hook up at night when they were both rostered on together.

I would also spend time with Doris's son, Nick. He was a little older than me but somehow we seemed to get along really well. Doris's husband had passed away some years prior, and without extended family I mainly saw the two of them.

I was still quite young when Betty passed away, leaving Doris as the sole cleaner at 3 The Ridgeway. I remember her being a smoker, outspoken and extremely supportive of me and my sister.

# SOME OF THE OTHER EIGHTEEN KIDS I SHARED THE HOUSE WITH!

## Gary

Originally from Nigeria, Gary was always one of the older boys and one I looked up to. As far as I was concerned he embodied everything that I thought I wanted to be. With a stocky build and great body he was a good-looking guy. He also had an arsenal of lyrics to entice any woman if his physical prowess ever failed him. When it came to sport, he excelled in anything that involved hand–eye ball coordination. In fact, even in those pastimes that didn't involve hand–eye ball coordination, such as dancing, martial arts and boxing for starters, he still managed to blow me away. What I appreciated about him most was the amount of time he'd spend with me teaching me the finer points of football, table tennis and volleying in tennis.

I remember one of my most embarrassing moments involved Gary; well actually there were two which stand out amongst many. As a very young kid, I was standing in the corner shop that was 300 metres from the home. I was busting to go to the toilet, but was too shy to say as Gary was talking to someone, I think it was the store owner, and I didn't want to interrupt. So there I was, standing in silence with the point of no return quickly approaching. I started tugging at Gary's leg, gently at first, but as the seconds rolled past my tugging became more furious! Finally he turned around and said 'What?' Alas, by this time it was too late, the chain reaction had already started, and I couldn't actually speak even if I wanted to. I could feel uncomfortable things happening down there in my never regions. The more I tried to hold it the more it came out – it was like trying to close the barn doors when the horse had already bolted! My concentration was sharply interrupted as Gary said out loud 'Bonnick, did you shit yourself?' I felt all the attention focused on me for all the wrong reasons, as that unmistakeable smell began to waft in and fill the shop. Have you ever tried to walk 300 metres or so with a problem that's spreading in your underwear? It was a long, slow, truly awful walk home.

The other incident was equally as embarrassing but much less, noxious and public… I think!

As you may remember, the first floor of our three-storey home had a landing and two full length reinforced glass windows either side of the door (made out of the same glass). The glass door was effectively a sound barrier to the rest of the house, as after entering this door you dovetailed into the long, narrow corridor running from left to right, as I explained earlier. At night-time you could switch off the light coming up the stairs, then close the full-length glass landing door behind you. If you switched on the light inside the long narrow corridor you'd have a full-length reflection in the full-length glass door and windows either side. The only challenge was that you couldn't see through to the other side!

Standing there with the door to the boys' room open and a sound system on, you now had the makings of a small dance studio with mirror. I'd seen Gary dance and I wanted to emulate his dance moves, so I practised the cool, slow shuffle he did with a turn, a pirouette of sorts. I practised the hand and arm positions, straight down the sides of my body towards my knees. I executed the weight transfer from right to left leg, and back again, whilst keeping my head straight, and my toes pointing upwards. I can't say how long I was there for, but it was a while! At some stage I got 'that' feeling – you know, the one where it feels like someone is watching you! I was having such a great time being in zone that I didn't even see, Gary himself, standing in the darkness behind the door, watching my every move! I got the fright of my life when that glass door, my mirror for goodness sake, suddenly opened to reveal his smiling, somewhat entertained face.

I idolised Gary, and being a martial arts/boxing legend sealed his epitome of cool to me! There was only one time of any serious note in which I felt he let me down, which was to do with my ex-girlfriend, but that's another story.

In the later years of 3 The Ridgeway, his penchant

for gastronomy, producing some masterful, unbelievably delicate creations of such technique it defied logic, landed him some serious success. He was to become probably the first black head chef at one of London's top restaurants, and at the time of writing this book he controls the reigns at The Ivy restaurant in London and is about to launch his own book too.

### Ivan

I could never understand where Ivan came or descended from! Yes he was black, but more than that, he was a tallish man standing just shy of 6 feet tall, but he didn't look it due to his sturdy, burly frame. He was powerfully built and well proportioned; to say he was muscular would be a tremendous understatement! He was a sprinter and not just any sprinter, but he became one of the top sprinters in the country. I remember going to Crystal Palace to watch him sprint the 100 metres. I wish I could find some of his personal best times but I can say he was unbelievably quick! What I can say is that he went toe to toe with his strongest rival, Mike MacFarlane; from memory I think Ivan beat him on occasion too. Mike MacFarlane was the predecessor to the mighty Linford Christie, who was World Champion in the late 1980s and 1990s.

I was always scared of Ivan. He had an overpowering nature and he carried an aura that was stern and not to be trifled with! He didn't feel compelled to soften his fierce demeanour by smiling much either. He was always his own man! Being one of the oldest there during my stay, I don't really recall being close to him for the majority of the time. Only years later, after I had left the 3 The Ridgeway, did I actually realise I had misunderstood who Ivan was and what he stood for. Yes he was fierce but in the world we grew up in, especially as a black man, if you weren't you would be brushed aside.

Ivan moved into the public education system after his sprinting days were over, initially as a physical education teacher. He rose through the system becoming a sport centre manager, followed by various roles in local and regional government and up through the political structure of policy making, which sat above it, like a specially convened panel of experts.

One day I asked for his help and advice regarding a job opportunity. Advising me what to do caused us to spend more time together and over this period of time, I realised here was a man who'd seen the frailties and failures of the education system and decided to do something about it instead, like many, of just sitting back and complaining about it. I wouldn't go as far as to say he was a humanitarian but he was entirely adverse to supporting a structure which didn't possess equity and common sense and which also comprised elements of racism. He was his own man and I respected him highly. But there was a price to pay, in that I believe his health and relationships suffered as a result of his dedication and work ethic.

### Raymond and Stephen

Raymond was the elder of the two brothers, who were both

older than me (then again everyone was), and sported well shaped afro hairstyles. Both brothers always had a well placed afro comb on hand and from memory Stephen's was often sticking out the back or the side of his afro, whilst Raymond had what I could only describe as a back pocket thing going on. One of them had a really well maintained, cool of the time pair of Adidas Gazelles. They were both great sportsmen in their own right and I learnt much from them. Raymond was the more low-key of the two and didn't speak much, but when he did, you listened. He was more often than not, well thought out and deliberate.

Stephen didn't have this burden; that man could talk!! Smooth like butter is how I'd describe him, but he also had a tendency to take things just that little bit too far; a 'stirrer' would be a modest understatement. He would, could and often did tease you till the point past annoying, for example, teasing my sister Carol about the unsightly birthmark on her leg, which really did cause a lot of pain unfortunately. But Stephen would also comfort me when I was in need, perhaps if some of the other boys were picking on me. I loved Stephen dearly too, as I came to love all the long stayers at 3 The Ridgeway.

### A family feeling!

Between all the boys at 3 The Ridgeway was a kind of subtle elixir of love which pervaded the teasing, the bullying, the playing up, but also the hours spent playing football, tennis and basketball together. I bunked off (truancy) from school, sneaked out way past bedtime to go to all-night house parties and would come back before my absence was noted in the early hours of the morning, and we'd cover for each other.

On a few occasions (taking it in turns), in the dead of night we'd unleash the black widow catapult! This was no ordinary catapult! It was lightweight yet sturdy with a brace that hugged and supported most of your forearm. It had a recoil that would rock you back on your feet if you weren't concentrating. The procedure was as such: open the window of the boys' room, which looked down onto the street and the bus shelter below and opposite – we are talking some distance, 30 to 40 metres or more away. Put a small stone into the canvas projectile holder, pull back and hold. Take aim then, pull back some more, feeling the tension rise like a thick, reinforced elastic band about to snap. Then unleash. The projectile travelled with such velocity and the impact had such ferocity that it took out the glass bus shelter opposite our house. It was like a gunshot! Even car alarms were triggered, without doubt waking up our fellow housemates, neighbours and the police alike. A short time later we'd hear one of the staff members thumping around upstairs like a giant before thundering downstairs (you could feel every step). Quick! Close the window. Hide the catapult. Jump in bed and pretend to be asleep. With almost as much force as the glass shattering, the door of our bedroom flung open with one pissed off member of staff who was on duty looking for the guilty assailant or assailants. Rarely did they know who did it!

## Yes, we were punished too!

There were some occasions when we were not so fortunate, and to this day I still don't know what gave us away, but the catapult was confiscated, the conspirators were rounded up and summarily dealt with, a number of torturous techniques kept for the worst offences.

All I'm going to say is that we were in the time before physical punishment was outlawed, shunned or look disapprovingly upon. For swearing I remember washing my mouth out with soap and water, worse than that, the striated soap from Shield. It was just too big to fit comfortably into the largest of mouths, let alone mine. It tasted quite fruity upon entry but after the enzymes of the salivary glands kicked in it took on a very different taste, and I was being watched by a member of staff so couldn't take it out. I just wanted to throw up; it was horrible. I remember receiving the slipper quite a few times on the backside, hard enough that it hurt to sit afterwards. As I'm talking about sitting, one of the worst, which wasn't physically abusive, was being forced to sit on the stairs till I inevitably fell asleep and woke up in bed. Those steps leading upstairs from the living room on the ground floor were cold, hard and draughty! There were times if I didn't eat my food it was left and reheated for the next meal – I don't remember my record but it wouldn't surprise me if it went on to the next day or days; by that age, early teens probably, I was stubborn too. Ironically, I was feeding my three-year-old yesterday and she asked for a bottle of milk, which I happily gave, but it came back half drunk! Well I guess it triggered old memories. Luckily I didn't need to reheat it for the next mealtime, even though she is so stubborn. I wonder where she gets that from?

### Stephen

I don't think Stephen meant to go too far, teasing my sister especially, I just don't think he was aware of his depth, of how his actions affected her. But he was cheeky; here's one further example I already mentioned earlier in passing. I was young, impressionable and wanted to please (I'm probably still like that) and Stephen had this milk round going – or was it paper round? Probably both – I did both! I used to get up really early to help him, more than likely I probably offered at first, after which he'd wake me up knowing I wouldn't say no. I used run around delivering milk door to door whilst he drove and got paid and I didn't. Years later he told me that he felt bad about not paying me (we're talking over years here) but I didn't complain so he didn't bring it up – like I said…cheeky!

### Conrad

He was another of the older ones, who bore no relation to Gary, despite having the same surname. He wore thick rim spectacles and he always had a vibe about him of 'if you mess with me or poke fun at me, well you're going to get hurt.' It felt like I was only one misplaced joke away from receiving a beating! He grew up to be another kung-fu or martial arts king – no surprises there! He was one of the boys who shared our boys' room. I remember he would snore loudly at night-time – though you wouldn't tell him that or you'd be in danger of him throwing you a beating! He would sleep in a single bed less than 2–3 metres away from me and the bunk bed I'd sleep in. So scared was I of the 'LBC' radio channel come 'news time', which is what he used to fall asleep listening to at night-time, I would get out of my bunk, crawl under his bed, reach my arm up and switch it off. This was no mean feat for me as I was scared of the dark!

## Lee

Lee had a precocious quality and nature about him. He was a true rebel. He regularly smoked joints (he wasn't the only one back then) and spoke his mind without fear of reprimand. Tossed around from children's home to children's home, I don't think he got a chance to really connect with a father figure, and that was a shame. I don't recall him treating me badly, or any other orphan that I could remember, but he gave the members of staff hell. I was much younger so the opportunities for us to speak were limited. If we did find an opportunity to speak it would be him telling me about the need to stick up for myself.

He carried himself with an air of self-empowerment, like he knew best and no-one would ever tell him what to do. He fiercely opposed being controlled or manipulated in any way and took a healthy distrust of the establishment or anyone who represented that, as far as I could see. He had some traits that I envied – he just seemed so self-assured and powerful and had a cockiness to him that made being like him even more appealing. Part Jamaican, it seemed, though very light skinned and slight of build, he wasn't a tall man, though that didn't seem to deter him for one second from being his own man. He walked with a limp and to this day I'm not sure whether it was to alleviate an injury or just part of his swagger! To make up for the limp and stabilise himself he had a cane with a beautifully ornate handle. It may have been gold! This just added to his 'coolness'. I wish my memory served me better but I also believe he was a hit with the ladies too. I remember a photo taken with him Gary and a few of the other boys. They called themselves the DB Posse for short, which stood for double-breasted posse, and yes, they were cool!

I loved Lee too but his life was to meet a shocking, untimely and unexpected demise – if only one person could have connected with him perhaps he'd still be with us today.

### Darren

Darren was nearest in age to me out of everyone at 3 The Ridgeway except Dulcie, who arrived much later when 3 The Ridgeway had almost closed its doors for good after being sold to a developer. Now the prestigious 3 The Ridgeway has given way to a bunch of neo-modern apartments.

Darren was Caucasian, and while he wasn't the only one, over the years that I was there the number of black or brown skins outweighed whites significantly. But then, by way of improving the mix we had Turkish, Mauritian, Indian, German, Afghan, Greek and mulatto as well.

There were more racial eccentricities but these are all that I remember; a large, truly multicultural family many of whom had spent time inside (jail) as well! Even though I haven't mentioned much about them, there were also plenty of females there too – Carol, Brenda, Jackie, Janet, Dulcie to name but a few – but my life there was really about the boys. Though I have to say, because I was a very shy kid, I wanted to be like the older boys but didn't have the confidence and consequently found deeper friendships with females.

Back to Darren, I mentioned the colour cross-section as I think it has significance as far as he was concerned. From memory he was a problem child and had some close shaves with the law, and in some cases ended up on the wrong side of it. Though not an academic (I'm hard pushed to find anyone who was in 3 The Ridgeway) he wasn't slow either. I'd say the school of hard knocks paid him repeated visits. Perhaps it was the lack of white role models, or his background of falling into the wrong company, but at some stage he became a Neo-Nazi or skinhead. If memory serves me correctly Brian of 'The Mods Are Coming' fame (later in the book) was in fact a not-so-sharp friend of his. This led to a bit of a predicament. Philosophically he was a skinhead, which meant that he probably wouldn't really consort with or befriend, for example, blacks. Not only did he do that – remember, he still was one of our family! – but he lived with us too. In any case, in the early days there was a period of time when he and I were made to bare-knuckle fight in the boys' room on Saturday mornings, unbeknownst to the staff (of which there were many things). The fights would usually start off well for me, having a slightly longer reach, until a punch was landed on my nose (I wasn't really much of a fighter). As blood started to pour the fight was stopped and I'm pretty sure Darren crowned the winner. I can't remember if I ever won back then!

I still wonder what became of him; I worry about him.

### Dulcie

Younger than me by a year or so, Dulcie was a tomboy, street smart, quiet, yet had a lot to say, with a great body. She was controversial, bold, to the point, and quick to stand up for herself. Actually she really didn't take any of the proverbial – from anyone. She seemed to abhor authority figures and all that authority stood for. Sounds like Lee and she was a remarkable girl. Let me give you an example. Right at the end when we (my sister, Dulcie and I) were the only kids left officially at the 3 The Ridgeway, the confidential file kept on all of us during our time of being 'in care' was kept upstairs in the office in between either the locked filing cabinet or on the desk if the file was being amended. We all knew we had this file, all of us had seen elements of ours, even added little snippets and what not to it over the years. It stood as a documentation, the history of our time in care, but also went so much further down the rabbit hole than that, as it kept a record of every school report, sports report, medal ceremony, problem with the police or authorities, birth certificate information, details of our social workers, our families, how we came to be in care in the first place, it had names, addresses, dates and times. It was everything...the proof that we had existed at all! In the final days of our time at 3The Ridgeway we had a chance to use the not-so-official route of acquiring this file once and for all. Dulcie took that opportunity from the office upstairs when the file was available. It may have been that she had found the key and opened it herself and effectively stole it or simply that it was left out as it was being amended and she just helped herself. She advised me to do the same. Suffice to say, I didn't follow, and little did I know that thirty years later I would finally 'officially' get a hold of that document. In hindsight, I should have followed Dulcie! I hope if she reads this that it will make her smile! You were right Dulc!

# CHAPTER 7

# WHAT DID AN AVERAGE DAY LOOK LIKE?

I've already shared some insights into what some of my life was like growing up in 3 The Ridgeway. I'm doing this so you get a picture of where I came from compared to where I ended up. In many ways I've included more of the happy stories so far and not the sad ones, but stay tuned, as I'll reveal some of those too. I have a very good friend Judi (my unofficial adopted mum) who put forward the idea of telling the story of what it was like growing up in a children's home, as many people haven't experienced it before and may find it interesting. In many ways I take it for granted as I lived it.

I was not even two years old when I first reached 3 The Ridgeway and almost eighteen years of age when I left so to describe an average day is very challenging as it was constantly changing based upon the number of kids there, relative ages, which members of staff were rostered on and whether it was a weekday or weekend. So what follows is based more about my feeling of what happened.

## Weekdays

The home was set up in a way to mimic a normal family living environment. This also changed as I became older. In the early years, to the best of my knowledge, I would wake up early and would end up helping Stephen with some type of paper/milk round before going to school. Breakfast was on the fly, and as I would be returning as everyone else was getting up, a more formal breakfast of cereal, toast, jam, fried eggs and bacon would be prepared by whichever members of staff were on. Call it a typical English breakfast. Chingford Infant and Chingford Junior High Schools were all in a good walking distance so I'd be walking with someone early on, and by myself as I became older.

We had a morning break between classes followed by a longer lunch break at school, or quick one at home, then back again before lunchtime was over. The afternoon session was really a case of holding my breath, like most kids, until that FINAL BELL could be heard then I would run for my life out of school to get home again! Once again not a crazy different experience to most, I would have thought, at this stage. Immediately after reaching home I'd change out of my uniform, shower and change into some more comfortable clothes. When I reached junior and senior high, after school was taken up with sporting activities, such as football, basketball, cross country and tennis.

Evening comprised a dinner with everyone* together around our big dinner table, with the members of staff who were 'on shift' for that night. The members of staff would take it in turns to cook. Eugene, Geoff (most likely Monty) brought a more West Indian flavour whilst other members of staff cooked the type of cuisine that the English palate would appreciate more. Personally I used to really love the rice and beans (Jamaican) dishes – packed full of flavour!

The next challenge was TV-watching time, where most of us would be hunkered down in the large living room. The person who determined what we were watching was based on a pecking order and I was typically way down the bottom. The pecking order was based upon age/personal power so the older you were, in many ways the more freedom you were granted, and the opposite for the likes of the youngest (me). I even had to go to bed first, at the earliest time too. Depending what age I was and which staff member was on would determine whether I'd stall to be the first to go to bed. I'd try playing up, getting in trouble, causing trouble, hiding, or another brilliant tactic (which as dazzling as I thought they were usually didn't work). This could very well mean that I'd be sat on the stairs as a punishment and go to bed only after some of the older ones had already gone to bed.

*If you were one of the older ones, towards the end of my stay at 3 The Ridgeway, instead of meals being made for you, you would be put on a 'budget'. The easiest way to describe it is like living in a share house. I'd receive an amount of money to shop for food each week and would have to store and cook it myself. This was part of the way in which you were able to prepare yourself for living alone after you left.

As I mentioned, I was scared of the dark and I was in a bunk bed in furthest, darkest corner of our boys' room. Therefore, unless I was really tired and knew I'd fall asleep immediately and wake up when some of the other boys were already snoring away, I didn't want to be up there by myself!

## Weekends

An average weekend day was much the same except NO SCHOOL! and bedtimes were so much more relaxed, as I could get away with getting to bed later as I had no school to get up for, both of which were fine by me! I still had the paper or milk round to do but I think I enjoyed being of service more than anything else. As mentioned before, most weekends we'd have a whole bunch of people come around and play football in the backyard and I remember on some occasions Gary or Stephen would teach me tennis skills. Another very positive thing about my time there was that I received a great deal of free sports coaching, probably more than my fair share really. But just about everyone was fiercely competitive and didn't like losing in any sport they played.

## Living two lives

I felt like I was living two lives, and in my home life I was very shy and constantly aware of my surroundings, in which I didn't really feel that safe all the time, especially during my younger years. From my school reports, via my confidential file reviews, all the makings of this existed and I needed a lot of work and affection. It seems as a child

I knew where to find this affection, that is, who felt like the safest person to go to. This didn't necessarily mean the members of staff per se either. Sometimes it would be the cleaners, and as I grew up it became other people's parents too.

### The box out game...adding insult to injury!

When I was older, with pocket money in hand, I was running excitedly down the stairs thinking about what I was going to spend it on, when suddenly, I'm waylaid midway down by one of the older the boys. I stop and look up at who it is. My money is still in my hand as I haven't yet put it in my pocket. As I look up I feel another hand slap the underside of mine, releasing into the air the contents of what's held inside it, my pocket money! Still too small to fight, I am a victim of the 'box out' game. Like playing 'it' in kiss chase or the seeker in hide and seek, except the consequences were far worse. I'd wait all week! Sometimes I'd save up for weeks in a row delaying my gratification till I was ready to buy that treat for myself. Then, in a blink of an eye one of the older boys would 'box out' the money in my hands and whatever he'd pick up he could keep. It reminded me of the feeling when I first arrived and was bullied by the older kids for sucking my fingers and making too much noise during TV-watching time.

### Life outside 3 The Ridgeway

As the years went on, my life became more about what was happening outside 3 The Ridgeway. Inside I regularly felt 'on edge' and on the lookout for the others; was I about to be bullied or about to become a victim of the box out game? I began to realise I had a natural aptitude for sport, notably great hand–eye ball coordination, and soon realising this could be my way out. I began to develop a swagger of sorts, not in an egotistical way, but I enjoyed being good at something and I also enjoyed the adulation that it brought – okay so maybe a bit of ego! I also found it cathartic; whatever was going on at home I could exorcise on the sports field. Whatever was uncomfortable at home, I could put to the back of my mind. Little did I know I was becoming an introverted extrovert. At home I was an introvert, on the sports field at school an extrovert. The older I became the more apparent this was, and with increasing success this chasm grew wider still.

## More punishments

It's still hard for me remember a lot of things that happened growing up at 3 The Ridgeway – it feels like I missed so much. Acquiring my confidential file helped enormously, but I know some of the points which come next I wouldn't find documented anyway. Documenting them would incriminate those who were front and centre. I also had a brief conversation with a long-standing member of staff who was adamant that the punishments I recall didn't occur on her watch. Perhaps they took place before she started working at 3 The Ridgeway, or on the shifts that she was not present, or perhaps they even occurred in the St Barnardo's children's home that I was in from six months of age until being moved to 3 The Ridgeway. In any case, I do remember them.

For the period of time between sucking my fingers (when I was first admitted to the 3 The Ridgeway) and beginning to stand up for myself, anger played its part in my general daily make up. This anger would come frequently in bouts until just before my teens.

## My state of mind at that time

Many emotions were flying around within me that I couldn't really make any sense of. It was becoming increasingly apparent I wasn't going anywhere and 3 The Ridgeway was where I'd be staying for a while. Even though I saw my mother, who would frequently visit, it was also clear that she didn't have the capacity to look after my sister and I. I'll refer you to another entry in my confidential file below and transcribe part of it here also:

> It was stated that both children do not talk now about going home as they both have a realistic understanding of their life situation (as much as possible for their ages) in a sense they know that their Mother is unable to care for them although this maybe a great desire of hers A desire which she cannot because of her unstable mental condition, put into practice.

Since going back to being a nuclear family had become a pipe dream – or perhaps it was the normal rebellious nature of a boy at my age – I would play up. These are some of the punishments I remember.

## Swearing

As I mentioned previously, I remember having my mouth

washed out with soap and water using the thick bar of the striated Shield soap. I can still taste that soap even now. It goes in easy, though I have to open my mouth as wide and high as I can. It's not too unpleasant, actually tastes quite fruity at first. But as it is sitting there taking up a huge piece of real estate in my mouth, I can feel my salivary glands starting to kick in. Even though I know I have a bar of soap in my mouth my saliva glands keep on producing more waves of fluid. Every fibre of my being wants to spit the whole thing out but the member of staff won't let me. I know I don't want to swallow either or I would definitely vomit!

I don't think it was ever in for a long period of time, neither do I remember actually vomiting, but it was long enough for me to understand I really didn't want it in there again. I don't really recall the number of times I paid the price of this punishment but what I can say is that I don't miss it one bit!

### Uncle Jim and his slipper!

This took place back in the days when adults were allowed to strike children, such as a ruler over the knuckles, a cane to the backside or to the palms of the outstretched hands or applied to the soles of bare feet. As a parent to two young babies, I can agree they know the buttons to push, as they were the ones who installed them in the first place! These little terrors push you so far past your threshold of patience that even the most caring parent can lose it! So you can only imagine having to look after eighteen of us, each with our own eccentricities, baggage and ways of seeing the world. For some, 'the world hates me', for others, 'no-one loves me or cares for me, I'm on my own', or even 'the world owes me'. Over my years there I saw so many kids come and go. In hindsight I could see their 'theme tunes' as clear as day. I can't say I could blame them either, given some of their backgrounds and life experiences.

Therefore, when a member of staff was faced with some type of insubordinate behaviour what could they be expected to do? They probably had no way of dealing with it constructively. Experience gives you the knowledge to understand where these kids have come from and what they've endured – just check their confidential file! But what of the kids who didn't stay long; they didn't always want to be healed, related to or loved, depending on the theme tune playing loudly in their heads.

But, I digress. There were also times I recall being hit with the slipper for playing up, which was painful, at first. The interesting thing about pain is how you can switch it off or redirect it at someone or something else. Early on I developed within myself a kind of compartment within a compartment where I wouldn't let anyone in. Here I would hide my most sensitive, vulnerable, explosive findings about myself that I wanted no-one else to know. I could only trust myself. I was born alone and I'd die alone – that was my theme tune! It didn't matter what happened to me, how much bullying, teasing, smacking, cruel words or actions, they'd never reached that place. So when I played up and threw tantrums, sometimes it would be Uncle Jim's slipper that would pay me a visit. There I would be slumped forwards, stomach over the spin dryer, and hit repeatedly with a slipper to the backside. It hurt to sit down or walk for a time afterwards.

### Bed wetting

There was a practice at The Ridgeway that whenever you wet your bed you were not given any help to remake it or dress yourself. Also, you were given a cold bath! I later understood this changed when Gail took the reins. I look back in disbelief that I was punished in this way as I told some of the staff that I was afraid of the dark and that was why I wet the bed in the first place! Instead, they put me to bed in a bunk bed at the far corner of the boys' room, furthest away from the door, then switched the lights off and closed the door. Here's what would happen: I would pull the sheet or duvet over my head for safety and lie there barely breathing and begin to sweat. Every so often I poked my head out, quickly, to get some oxygen. I also peeked out into the darkness outside at the same time. I looked to where the door should be and then it would start. In front of my eyes I'd see the wardrobes move and morph into weird, imposing, scary shapes. Then my subconscious took over. What other demonic, scary or frightening creatures might there be out there? I'd go back under the covers and by this time I'd be hyperventilating. It was a vicious circle; the more I hyperventilated, the more oxygen I used, the more oxygen I used the quicker I ran out of air under the cover and the sweatier I became. I now needed to poke my head out from under the covers again but I'd open my eyes, get scared and dive back under the covers, and so on. I was too scared to leave the bunk bed and would think of ghost stories and horror movies, making matters worse.

As I was too scared to get out of bed and go to the toilet, I was faced with wetting the bed, having the light turned on, and the walk of humiliation carrying my wet bed linen through the house (later being teased for doing it) and down the stairs to the laundry, which would be followed by a cold bath. Otherwise I would face death by the malevolent forces of my darkest imaginations. Wetting the bed was the go-to-option almost every time!

To avoid all the above I would circumvent the process by not going to bed in the first place, or if I couldn't manage that, after being escorted to the bedroom, before fear took hold, I'd get up and run back downstairs to the TV room again and hide. Either way, I can't recall getting away with it even once! The usual punishment was to sit on the stairs.

## Sitting on the stairs

As described earlier, there were three levels at 3 The Ridgeway, with the landing on level one. I used to have to sit either on the first set of stairs directly outside the living room, or up the second flight of steps, closer to the landing. The stairs were uncomfortable, cold and draughty, as they also acted as the main conduit for the wind making its way up and down the stairs. The pyjamas I used to wear were not of a sufficient thickness to stave off the cold in any case. The other older boys and girls would walk past me on their way up the stairs to bed. But all in all this was a lighter punishment to serve, as opposed to facing the darkness in the bedroom by myself. Also, it did make me reflect on how I ended up there in the first place. Perhaps this is where I started meditating!

Sometimes I would fall asleep and wake up in bed to the familiar sounds of some of the other boys tossing, turning and snoring. It felt safe as I didn't feel like I was alone, dealing with the creatures of the dark my subconscious created.

### Staying out late sneaking in early!

As I became old enough to stay over at friends' houses (mid-teens and later) I'd go out to parties but was often given a curfew. Usually I adhered to the curfews but sometimes there would be too much good going on! Take house parties for example. The time I had to leave to get home punctually would always be synchronised to when the party was just getting going! I couldn't leave in that moment! This was especially true during the 'house party' or 'club' phenomena of the eighties. I would be economical with the truth some of the time and say to the member of staff on duty that I was sleeping over at a friend's house.

At house parties in those days you brought your own alcohol; cider, red stripe beer, thunderbird (snakebite), or a very cheap wine that tasted good on the way in, but gave you the worst headache the next day, on the way out. The house or flat where the party was held typically had been gutted of all of the furniture etcetera, which was all stored in one room and locked! The kitchen was always the most popular area initially, probably due to being where the alcohol was. The next thing you'd notice would be the absence of light. Damn these parties were dark! And the clientele were mainly black so in some rooms all you saw were teeth and eyes! You were always bumping into someone in the narrow corridors or small rooms. Heaven forbid if you needed to go to the toilet. The next thing I would notice would be the music; some of the best I've ever heard – a mix of beats, rhythms and melodies that allowed the occupants of the entire room to synchronise and dance as one. Lucky really, as it was usually an incredibly small space. The music was driven from one room, probably the living room, and filled the rest of the space via a ghetto blaster, midi hi-fi in the corner of the dark room. Occasionally if the host had means there might be Technics SL1200s, a mixer, amplifier, subs and tweeters.

Normally these parties were put on by friends, or friends of friends, no guest list just 'blagging' your way in if you weren't invited. By blagging I refer to dropping someone's name to the security (an imposing dude who either owned or rented the place, or a friend entrusted to do the same) with such conviction that you would get in.

So the scene was set: music, alcohol, venue, and I'm missing one important thing…the people! For a reason unbeknownst to me these parties were usually 70 per cent male and 30 per cent female, and I'm being generous! The odds would usually be even worse.

And so it continued into the early hours, or even daylight if the police didn't bring it to a premature close. I never recalled there being any trouble at these house parties; everyone just got along! Alpha males would be alpha males of course, using all their guile to 'pull' or 'get off with' one of the few girls on offer.

On one occasion that lucky guy was me.

Please, you have to understand I was a very shy guy when it came to women; I'm sure I was the oldest to lose my virginity around the males I had to contend with at 3 The Ridgeway. Females were my best friends outside the children's home, I found solace and confided greatly in women, but when it came to romantic involvement, unfortunately this was not the case. Let me give you an example that happened around the same time in my late teens. There was a gorgeous girl called Nikki who really did have all of the attributes I was attracted to in a girl: funny, didn't take herself too seriously, positive, warm to be around, intelligent, with a beautiful body. Once or twice a week she would take me for a drive in her car into Epping Forest (not too far away). We'd stop in the middle of nowhere, switch off the car and talk, talk, talk and talk some more! After a while the keys were returned to the ignition and we'd drive back to school, Nevin Drive in Chingford at that time. This continued for the entire year, if not longer! Fast forward some years to when I had left Chingford, travelled and lived in another part of Europe. I had returned to Chingford for a short time before going

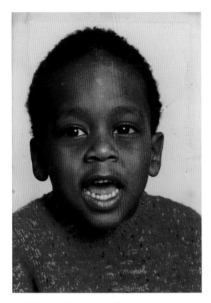

A picture of me when I was very young – you can see the 'peanut head' already developing!

My big Sister Carol who, little did I know at the time, always had her eye on me, as only a protective big sister could.

I think I remember this one and trying not to laugh. My sister had a great smile so it seems right to at least see a flash of those pearly whites.

I really like this photo of Aunty Gail. This one was taken on one of our holidays, camping in La Rochelle, France.

A special man indeed. Monty on one of our camping holidays to La Rochelle in France.

I really love this picture of (left to right) Uncle Tony, Aunty Lil and Aunty Gail.

A rare moment of Eugene not wearing her glasses whilst chilling out on one of our summer holidays.

Aunty Linda and my adversary (but brother-in-arms over the years) Darren. Taken outside one of our tents whilst on holiday in France.

A great shot of Aunty Leslie.

I'm sure this shot of Uncle Tony could be used for a Fred Perry Campaign.

A classic photo indeed of Gary and my sister Carol. This was the garden shed at the bottom of our back garden, behind the swings, i.e. the makeshift goal for football at the weekends!

From left to right my big Sister Carol and Ivan.

From left to right, Brenda, Stephen, Conrad and Raymond playing in the sand on holiday (probably in France).

Conrad on expedition during our holiday in the beautiful Lake District.

The cool-looking Lee with a pint in hand on holiday.

Another one of my favourite 'on holiday' shots, from left to right, Brenda (I didn't tell you she was a rockabilly!), Gary, Lee and Darren.

A mischievous Darren on holiday up the coast in England.

The gorgeous Joanie on one of our holidays.

From left to right Raymond, Darren, me and Joanie.

From left to right Brenda, a rare smile from me, and my big sister Carol.

Me and Jackie – love this hug! Looking back, in some ways she was like an older sis.

overseas again and I went to a local wine bar, where I saw Nikki again. She looked as I remembered and I was still very attracted to every sense of her being, but this time I had enough 'truth serum', that is alcohol, in my system. At some stage I brought up the drives to Epping Forest we used to do and the attraction and unexpressed desires towards her. It was like a giant roller shutter grill came tumbling down, the lights came on, music stopped, everyone was ordered out, we're closed! It's quite amazing what can be conveyed in a look! I got the feeling she wasn't happy then out came the words along these lines: 'You're an idiot Rob. Why do you think I drove us into Epping Forest all those times, and you didn't make one move, not one!'

I wish there was a happy ending to that story about how we made up for all of those years of pent-up emotions during the rest of the time I had in Chingford, but alas, she now had a partner and despite my waxing lyrical she wasn't about to give up on her relationship for the night! That sums up how confident I was at that time when it came to being alpha male in the area.

So hopping back in time to that house party where I walked out during the early hours of the next day with a girl I managed to pull on my arm...the pride I felt after the years of failure, the years of looking at the other boys, especially Gary, picking up girls like water running out of the tap. It wasn't like I felt vindicated, but I felt part of the posse. Nothing ever happened with that girl, not even a kiss! I dropped her off at Walthamstow Central train station and came home. I never even saw her again. I don't think we even exchanged two words. I did run home, have a quick shower and pretend I'd come home hours before, slept and was just getting up when a member of staff asked how my night went.

For stunts like this, if I was discovered, I would be grounded for weeks and privileges more than likely revoked too. As it happens I found an entry in my file for one such occasion. The key worker was Auntie Lil and she was most displeased! This is the entry (I was fifteen years old):

> 6.5.1984 'Late home from a party and made numerous excuses which the staff did not accept.'
>
> 6.5.1984 'Stayed at Daniel Khan's for the night.'

Daniel was one of my oldest friends outside of the 3 The Ridgeway. He was one or two years older than me and was a huge corrupting force – we were as thick as thieves. His mum, dad and younger brother Simon lived a hop skip and jump away and they were held in high esteem by the members of staff at 3 The Ridgeway.

> 2.6.1984 'Robert asked for some money and to stay at Daniel's. Everything agreed with Mrs Khan. It was later discovered he went to a party arriving back at Mrs Khan's much later than arranged. Not at all repentant [there we go, bringing Catholicism into it again!] for his deceitful behaviour he was kept in the following two weekends.'

## Stealing

I remember when I was still little that our corner shop was

run by a very nice owner who was respectful towards all of the kids from 3 The Ridgeway. It was a typical corner shop at the time, comprising an almighty selection of products crammed to precision and great order into rows of tall narrow shelves.

I don't quite remember how it happened or who caught me but I took some lollies without paying for them. It wasn't that I was caught by the shopkeeper but one of the other kids at 3 The Ridgeway. I think I'd inadvertently stumbled across another unwritten law – you don't steal from your own! I remember the same law existed years later when my sister Carol and I moved out to a council flat together, the top floor of one of those large high rises, St Albans Tower on Chingford Hall Estate. Part of this estate was a no-go zone at night; people went there to score drugs, mug people, sometimes worse, but if people knew that you lived there (and of course kept yourself to yourself, showed no fear, and said hello to the 'right' people) you were never touched.

Back to the corner shop, no matter how small I was, that really had nothing to do with it as I knew I was doing the wrong thing. So the toughest part wasn't the stealing, consuming or the act itself, it was having to take back the remnants of what was left to the owner of the store, describing what I had done and apologising whilst looking him in the eye.

It certainly worked as I don't recall having stolen again!

# CHAPTER 8

# WHAT THE HECK IS BULLYING ANYWAY?

**B**eing the small child who came into the children's home sucking my fingers, as that initial report mentioned, I was 'too young to look after or stand up for myself verbally or physically.'

While the members of staff would try to look out for me, they couldn't be there all the time. When you're in a group environment where some external power is seeking to protect you, that can make you even more of a target, especially when those powers that be are not around.

Quite a few of the older kids were fighters, and great fighters at that, from kung-fu to judo and boxing. From early on Darren and I were forced to bare-knuckle fight some Saturday mornings. Taking place in the boys' room with the others cheering on I recall on occasion having some advice given to me on how to win (as I usually lost). I don't think these mini bouts lasted for long though. Usually a well-placed punch on my nose from Darren would cause my nose to bleed and I'd head off to the bathroom. Mini-bout over.

The connection I didn't make until recently was that at the same time or period my mini bouts with Darren were going on, I was practising what the older boys were trying to teach me i.e. to toughen up. The recipient was Dennis at school. I was probably somewhere between five and ten years of age so after Chingford Infants School and before Wellington Avenue Secondary School (also in Chingford).

The way I had it set up in my mind was that I was the protector. Being tall for my age, I was taller than most of those in the same year as me. The smaller kids would be bullied and would come to me saying Dennis is chasing me. He would arrive and I would stick up for the one being chased by practising the latest punch combo I learnt at home. Most of the time the fight would end with Dennis on the floor!

Every now and then I wouldn't have it all my own way and the latest combo wouldn't work and I would be the recipient of a beating. But something in me would still keep going, and most of the time I was known as being one of the hardest in my year. The times I did get beaten up eventually changed my attitude to, if you have strength it's better to conceal it.

# CHAPTER 9

## STUPIDITY AND THE SEARCH FOR INTELLECT

**P**robably my favourite chapter, as it really shows me in the best light (sarcastically speaking).

My favourite topic at school was biology, not necessarily because I wanted to become a biologist but a biochemist. Unfortunately my maths was atrocious which put paid to that idea but I still received my O (or Ordinary) Level and A (or Advanced Level) biology certifications. I loved biology due to the understanding it afforded of the world around us. Like what happens to the air we breathe in from the time it enters the body, the role of the mucous lining, gaseous exchange on a cellular level utilising the small air sacs called alveoli that increase the surface area. The role of the blood cells in its transportation to all reaches of the human body, pumped by the heart. Conversely, how carbon dioxide is pumped by the heart out of the body after it's extracted by gaseous exchange in reverse. Millions of complex chemical reactions happening simultaneously in the body keeping us alive without us even have to consider it. This kind of information consistently blew me away. It still does!

I wouldn't call myself accident prone but, between the ages of around four to thirteen, I was super intrigued by the, 'what would happen if?'

Let me give you an example, I would sit on the branch of our apple tree in the back garden some five or so feet from the ground by myself. I'd become intrigued by gravity and would drop items out of the tree and watch them hit the ground. Gravity. The force acting upon all things to give the same result I'd just witnessed. I'm not sure how long I was up there for, but it was a while, probably confused by how cats always managed to land on their feet. We had two cats and I remember that over the years and they went through hell – one stayed for many years, Becky, and the other probably had the good sense to run away.

So the thought process was long enough for me to consider, what if I dived horizontally out of the tree? I could in fact re-correct my trajectory in mid-air and control my descent landing on my feet! Clearly if you're reading this you have the good sense to know that I was deluded! I remember hurling myself off the branch with my head and body at the very least parallel with the ground. I also remember the pain of landing smack bang, head slightly first, followed by face then body, on the ground! It happened so quickly! My experiments should have stopped there but with equal aplomb and complete disregard for an F for failure from the last experiment, I continued and here are the ones I remember.

## Running into monkey bars

This was by far the most painful and set the tone for all the others and wasn't quite done on purpose! At school, like most kids I was obsessed with football (the world game, aka soccer to some). It represented another game the great British Empire had invented, soon to be overtaken by the rest of the world, with the exception of 1966 – the only time England won the World Cup. Every year on paper we have the strongest team, which fails to deliver, and instead we're left to lament with that great line of 'We were robbed' (again).

So Chingford Primary School was the venue. I was sprinting towards the corner trying to cross the ball to one of my teammates before the ball went out of play. I reached the ball in time and made my cross and I believe we scored a goal out of it. Unfortunately, what I didn't count on was my momentum after making the cross, taking me hurtling towards the corrugated iron monkey bars. Carrying too much speed, I was on a collision course and what's worse, I also tried to duck the piece of metal nearest to avoid impact to my head. Alas, by the time I ducked it was already at my head. From the outside looking in, it looked as though I deliberately head butted the metal monkey bar. The outcome however was the same – a great deal of pain, blood, concussion, hospital and stitches!

## Running into a lamppost

By now people at home were calling me peanut head; it was a nickname that stuck alright! The more I hit my head the more it came to resemble a peanut shape. I already had a permanent bump (and scar for that matter) and I still wasn't done yet!

Closer to thirteen years of age I was out jogging through North Chingford, Chingford Green to be precise, a beautiful green expanse which cut through towards Station Road, the main road in North Chingford which ultimately headed out of Chingford towards Chingford Plains and Epping Forest. It was also where the gorgeous church could be found (Perpendicular Gothic style). There were a number of perfectly and equally spaced lampposts on either side. Running with a buddy (I wish I remember who – maybe if they read this they will remember), at some stage I had the thought of 'what would happen if?' It wasn't difficult to line up a lamppost, as running at an even pace, the lampposts would be encountered after the same time due to their equal spacing.

Luckily I wasn't travelling that fast but was still carrying enough speed to make contact with my head and shortly thereafter my upper body and leg, the force of the impact sending me almost simultaneously to the ground on my back! It was quite painful but as I mentioned, by now my peanut head didn't really split open anymore; it had become a super-hard piece of reinforced super skull.

### Knife in the kitchen...

Perhaps I was around twelve to fourteen years of age or so when this one happened. Every now and again when I was still hungry I would sneak downstairs in the middle of the night and eat some snacks before returning to bed. Who knows what possessed me for this instalment of, 'I wonder what would happen if?' Throwing, spinning in the air and catching by the handle the normal knife I was using to butter my sandwich was by no stretch of the imagination a mean feat! But what came next, taking a large carving knife nine or ten inches long out of the drawer, to do the same thing would take a little more nerve and went something like this…

Feeling the weight of the handle and the blade I find the balance point. I prepare for the throw but don't release it. I just want to see how much power it takes to turn the blade in mid-air. I repeat the same process, only this time I have the balls to let the knife go. The handle rotates in, up and high into the air. I keep my eyes firmly locked on the knife's trajectory. I'm not breathing. My heart is in my mouth, a mix of excitement and fear. The knife is still up in the air rotating. Now it's past the halfway point on its first and single revolution. I can see the path of the handle of the blade coming straight back into my outstretched right palm. My eyes follow the handle until it reaches my hand! Phew I can breathe again as I make a perfect catch. I should stop now I think to myself, but it feels good. I am dominated by a mix of 'I shouldn't be doing this' and 'How good was that?' 'I have to prove it wasn't a fluke!' So I go again, this time with less trepidation. I go through the motions again. Carving knife handle, feel the weight, throw, release, spin and catch. The euphoria of the moment subsides each time I do it. I need a new challenge I think to myself. I know, a double revolution! I go through the same steps as before without interruption Carving knife, handle, feel the weight, and throw harder and higher this time. I realise now as it's spinning up that I may have thrown it too hard but know it's too late. It's out of control and I can't track its path. I'm in trouble. I freeze and lose track of the knife and it feels like, if I close my eyes it can't hurt me. Wrong! Though luckily for me the trajectory taken by my throw of the knife had led the knife to find a shallow resting position. Not on the floor, not in the sink or in my foot for that matter, but lodged in my shoulder! In the soft tissue behind the clavicle and in front of the scapula. To make matters worse a stream of blood was working its way calmly down the front of my chest. I still have the scar!

## Goalposts and kids running into me

By this time I had also run into goalposts and other people numerous times, so it only seemed natural to combine my ball skills in Rugby Union too. We went on a school rugby tour to the north of England. I played centre or 'crash' centre, as I was still tall for my age, not particular muscular, but on the field I had no fear. This meant that even though I was quick (but not the fastest on my team) when making tackles I came into them at speed and with momentum. The real reason wasn't so much absence of fear but anger. I was in my middle-to-late teens and I was angry. What infuriated me most was the chant the opposing fans and team kept repeating as we got off the coach, 'There's no Black on the Union Jack'.

I had faced racism before, as I was the only black kid at school for the first thirteen or fourteen years of my schooling. I was one of the best all-round sportsmen the school ever had and I won that medal numerous times so because of my sporting achievements I was given respect. I was also respected because of the older kids from the children's home who went before me at school and who everyone knew. So this was different and it really pissed me off!

That whole tour I played like a man possessed in the body of a teenager. Where I made a huge impact was in tackling. We were trained to tackle the classic way of shoulder into the thigh or below, then hold on for dear life until they fell. I was so irate I would go in 'peanut' first, straight into the side of the thigh. I would hit with such fury and impact my prey wouldn't get up…for a while! My teammates knew what I was like; I would line up front row, wingers and other backs alike. Anyone who gave me lip was in for a triple dose of impact. I was lucky not to break my neck!

Before we left the venue of that tour my opposition still may have not liked me or my skin colour but I had their respect! I approached almost every game like that especially after that tour, no matter the sport. I had something to prove each time whether there was racism present or not. I was even doing sliding tackles on concrete playing football during play times!

# CHAPTER 10

# THE MODS ARE COMING

For me racism, ignorance and stupidity have always gone hand in hand. By way of illustration, I remember on one occasion when I was in my early years watching TV in our front room with six or eight others, not too late in the day, when we heard someone yelling, 'The mods are coming, the mods are coming'. The person yelling this, from memory, was a man by the name of Brian. A skinhead, I wouldn't go as far as to say he was a Neo-Nazi despite the tattoos, braces and too-tight jeans which didn't quite reach the top of the 21-hole, steel-toe-capped Dr Martens he almost always wore. However, skinny and standing at over 6 feet tall with a huge tattoo that covered approximately half of his face, you could be forgiven for wanting to cross the road and walk on the other side of the street to avoid him. He looked menacing! From memory, he had done 'time' too, though he was still under eighteen. In reality, while I wouldn't go as far as to call him a big softy, that wasn't too far from the truth. I still wonder what happened to him! The children's home was a halfway house of sorts. The local wealthy types didn't really want a bar of us but that didn't stop the Brians of the world adopting us as their home away from home.

I wouldn't be at all surprised that 'the mods are coming' actually meant that they were giving chase to Brian at the time and had he run somewhere else there would be no need to share what comes next…crash!!! Something big came through our front living room window onto the carpet as we were watching television, shards of glass scattered everywhere, and panic ensued. All the kids ran upstairs as the full scale of what was unfolding became apparent; we were under siege from a gang of mods. Some on scooters, some on foot, others in cars, and they were 'tooled up' with batons and other implements. I remember seeing three or four of our guys (the older boys who by the age of eighteen were shipped off from the children's home, the state having done its duty, and you were now of adult age) who were mostly extremely good fighters. So even though the mods and entourage greatly outnumbered us, the ultimate victor of that battle was 3 The Ridgeway! Highlights that I remember were the young kids including myself throwing China cups from the tallest room in the house – the office, aka mission control – onto the mods below, the numerous phone calls to the police station less than 100 metres away and they still never came, and seeing the best of kung-fu, boxing and the sheer will to survive or win displayed by my fellow orphans. Towards the latter end of the battle – which maybe went on for ten or twenty minutes I was very scared – I remember seeing a mod on a Vespa coming up the pavement towards our front gate. Unbeknownst to him, which we could see from our elevated position, one of our guys was hiding behind the bush, twisted round with a chair cocked back behind him, like Roger Federer about to hit one of those flat-out backhand passing shots down the line, but waiting for the right moment to strike. When the strike finally came it was timed to perfection; the body that was driving the scooter crunched up on impact around the chair and remained suspended in the air whilst the Vespa, now driverless, whizzed off down the street and into the road. Priceless! A moment of hilarity amidst our feelings of helplessness and fear.

After the street fight in our front garden was well and truly over and most of the mods had escaped to lick their wounds the police arrived and tried to press charges on one of our guys for possession of an offensive weapon, which I think was a mop head! We were clearly not wanted by some in that neighbourhood.

# PART 3

# HOW I CAME TO DISCOVER THE FIVE KEYS, EARLY TRAGEDIES AND MIRACULOUS TURNING POINTS

# MORE FROM THE RIDGEWAY

### Racism

I was no more than fifteen years of age, at a stretch, and much had happened in the years at 3 The Ridgeway, but I was a person who saw the glass half full as opposed to half empty. I was overcoming my fears, doing well at school, had a large number of friends, was playing basketball for the England national team – I felt good about myself. But I still believed in the cowboys versus the Indians, that is, the cowboys were the good guys, the Indians the bad. Little did I know that illusion was about to be shattered!

Andy and I were walking past a pub in South Chingford, busily talking away about something or other. Andy was a handsome black guy a few years older than me. Smaller than me, he was wearing a Lyle & Scott diamond jumper, which at the time was one of the most highly respected and honoured pieces of merchandise around – even strangers would comment on it. He lived two stones throws away from our children's home with his younger brother Steven and his mum. He was a great guy Andy, quiet by nature with a wicked sense of wit, he had a great way with the ladies. He was cool, I liked hanging with him and he was well liked and trusted by all the staff at 3 The Ridgeway.

Whatever we were talking about was pierced suddenly by some good ol' ignorance: 'Oi Nigger! Go back to your own country.'

Running towards us, across the street from the pub, was a tall, lanky, hardly well-coordinated Caucasian man (most likely drunk). He came right up to my face yelling the same garbage. I told him I was born here and had the same right to be here. This didn't seem to land or matter as within a heartbeat I was on the floor, the result of one of his wayward punches. As I lay there in shock, I thought to myself I could fight, but something about fighting a fully grown man somehow scared me. But that didn't matter as this loudmouthed lout was the next to join the ground, care of a straight right from Andy. I forgot to mention Andy was a good fighter! I got to my feet but was scared, shocked and probably in the mammalian 'freeze' response. I remember seeing more Caucasian males coming out and Andy had engaged two more of them, but now a few more were chasing me. Now my 'flight' response was well and truly triggered! They didn't catch me and soon gave up the chase to run back to where Andy now was. I called out or gestured to Andy in some way that we should leave and quickly, which was unlikely at best. Andy was now curled up on the ground covering his head and about 8–10 Caucasian males were kicking him like one would kick a football, again and again and again. I was close enough to see but too far away for this 'educated' group of men to give chase to me. I can't tell you how scared I was, or how guilty I felt because I should be there too – in my mind Andy was getting 'a kickin'' for me, despite my screams to stop.

What happened next shattered my illusion of the Cowboys and Indians and fairness in the world, or absence of it, but at the same time left me with a tiny grain of hope too.

More men came running out of the pub. By now this one-sided affair was three minutes or so into its duration and no-one – passers-by, people from the pub – seemed like stopping it, or even wanting to. The next wave coming out, maybe out of desperation (mine) seemed like they were going to stop it but they just pushed the other guys aside to lay some fresh boots into Andy! Part of me just 'broke' inside; it's very difficult to put into words the feeling when you desperately hope something will happen and it's fair and reasonable for it to be that way but the opposite happens. After I had given up hope, a bunch of girls, perhaps girlfriends of some of the males, after they saw what was happening put them all to shame, the way only the energy of a matriarch can. I remember those words like it's yesterday: 'You ought to be ashamed of yourselves! Look how many of you there are compared to them! You should be ashamed of yourselves.'

This seemed to cause enough of an interruption for

Andy to get up and run. Together we made our haste.

Physically, Andy wasn't hurt too badly considering what had happened. Emotionally, I can't say; I'm not sure if we ever discussed it at any great length – I remember trying to apologise and him brushing it off in his own way. I remember him being more upset with the hole in his diamond jumper than anything else. But what really haunted me were the tears that came out of his eyes when he was explaining the story to one of the older boys at 3 The Ridgeway.

## Be an ambassador

From a very young age I always envisaged myself as an ambassador; I still do today. I wanted to be Kofi Anan, President of the United Nations, till I saw how the United Nations itself is flawed, as it appears whichever country contributes the most dollars seems to have a bigger say. I say this to give you an insight into how I view racism. To me it's based upon ignorance and fear. Take those away and it's just people relating to one another as human beings. One of the most important things 3 The Ridgeway taught me was how, despite coming from very different upbringings, ideologies and ways of life, we were still one family. We'd still stick up for one another and in many ways love one another. Racist acts like these upset me but all in all strengthened my resolve!

## Lee

As I said earlier on, my memory of Lee was that of an enigma, a force of nature, his own man. He lived life on his terms and he didn't stand for older establishment heads telling him what to do. On reflection, I think he needed a very strong, caring and understanding role model, not quite a father figure, more like an older brother who he respected and probably smoked spliff. I think Monty, one of my favourite members of staff, had the capacity to go there, but wasn't given enough latitude by the system of care of the day to really have a fighting chance. So due to this, I guess Lee was destined to fall through the cracks, with no safety net or parachute in sight. No-one there could control or have an impact on him except Ivan. But as that second photo shows, there was also another side to Lee. We didn't talk much apart from him telling me to be a man and step up, more like a big brother type role, in the words of Bob Marley, of whom he was a huge fan, 'Get up, standup, stand up for your rights. Get up stand up, and don't give it the fight.' In his more lucid moments it was clear to see that he cared about people. He cared about oppression, slavery and so much more. If he had made it, I wonder what kind of a person he would have become. But life had a different plan for Lee, one that I'm sure he never saw coming, a brutal, sudden and crushing way to extinguish a life of so much promise.

Lee was playing pool in the pub, a common and enjoyable pastime of the day. All the kids played too. We had snooker table at 3 The Ridgeway and the balls set up for both pool and snooker. Lee was a great player –I think he had his own cue too.

I'm unclear whether first a verbal altercation broke out between himself and his opponent, or someone else who happened to be there at the same time. It was clear at some stage this altercation escalated, it was clear it became physical and unfortunately for Lee a gun was exposed, brandished, pointed at him and at point blank range the trigger pulled. Lee was gone.

These were violent times the eighties and nineties but I hadn't heard so much of people being shot like that. All the dreams, aspirations, thoughts, conversations and so much more were gone – I don't even remember the last conversation we had; knowing Lee he probably would have had a spliff in his mouth with a remarkably laid-back, cool vibe going on.

Later it transpired, or perhaps it was just a story going around, that our Lee was involved in drug dealing and it was possibly a deal gone bad, turf war or a disgruntled customer. I don't really recall anyone talking at length about it at 3 The Ridgeway. We were all in shock. He was one of our own. No matter what he had or hadn't done nothing would change that fact.

It hit me hard and in my own time I wept for Lee. Later, as a result of his story – how he lived his life and how he died – I made a promise to myself at the deepest level that, whether he dealt drugs or not, I would never be involved in the dealing of drugs. Despite later spending twenty-plus years in the nightclub industry, where apparently drugs are rife, I never did!

## Jackie

My gut impression of Jackie was that of a kind and beautiful soul who never seemed to catch a break. She was very fair of skin with light red hair. Looking into her eyes felt like there was enough sadness, torment and unfairness to last a lifetime. She was tallish and attractive but it felt like she held herself small somehow. It is possible my memory is that of the moments she wasn't feeling happy or confident; perhaps that's why we got along, as some of the time I felt the same way. It wasn't as if we would hang out together and talk. I was still shy and young during those early years and she was far older. It was as though she needed more sun time, a good dose of lasting positivity and some good meals inside her, as she was quite thin too.

But over the years I did see her blossom. She had met, by all reports, a great guy called Peter who rode a sexy motorbike and lived close to the border of South Chingford, at the other end of The Ridgeway. The Ridgeway started very close to our home, a wide, statuesque type of a road with palatial abodes on either sides of it. If The Ridgeway was like a horse it would be a stallion! It wound its way a couple of miles or more from North Chingford to the large hill of Chingford Mount, where South Chingford started. To the north, not too far away you could get lost in Epping Forest, which was arguably one of the most beautiful natural forests in England. It was a great place to go pillion and I could understand why Jackie would look forward to this. If you have ever been on a motorbike in these kind of surrounds you couldn't be blamed for being just a bit envious – if the truth really be told, jealous! I could see that the members of staff feared for her safety, as they feared for the safety of all people on motorbikes, but they knew Peter was an experienced rider. I was out in the garden that day when the news came; we had lost another member of our family, Jackie, to an accident whilst on Peter's bike. Peter was not at fault. There had been some type of collision. Jackie was killed instantly and Peter was paralysed from the waist down.

Once again I wonder what would have become of Jackie had that awful accident not happened – she was just getting her life together, she was happy. It just seemed so senseless, random and unfair! What could you possibly take from that?

Years later I remember thinking about the impermanence of life itself; nothing seemed to be guaranteed. You could argue in the case of Lee, that his actions in some part were taking him on a journey with an inevitable destination – if he did what the rumours said. But Jackie? I couldn't see the same pattern or reasoning. As I searched for meaning and how to make some kind of sense of it all, 'enjoy every moment of your life as you don't know what may happen next' is what I took away with me after Jackie passed.

# CHAPTER 12

# ILLUSTRIOUS FRIENDSHIPS AND NEAR DISASTERS!

### Daniel

My best friend out of 3 The Ridgeway was older than me by a year or so. With a part Indian father and tall, attractive, English mother, it wasn't surprising that this guy cut a statuesque figure and was probably one of the most stunning looking men I'd seen. He was basically everything, at least socially, I felt like I wasn't; supremely confident, good looking, with the gift of the gab, knew how to talk to women, an incredible array of vocabulary to draw from – he surely must have aced English, and finally, he had the incredibly precise diction to back it all up. In short this guy was a catch! It seemed like women would fall at his feet like water would run from a tap…it was effortless! He embodied the good-looking alpha male, and I liked hanging out with him.

When it came to ball sports we were fiercely competitive, neither one giving ground easily, if at all. Sliding tackles whilst playing a so-called friendly five-a-side on the concrete playground would leave our trousers hole ridden and our knees bloody – but it was all about winning. The teammates on each side (we often played against each other) I suspect knew that they were pawns on a large board for Daniel and I to move as we pleased!

We actually got on pretty well socially (probably because he didn't see me as a threat) and from my early teens I'd spend nights sleeping at his house. He and his family presented so well that the staff at 3 The Ridgeway had no reason to be concerned. They probably should have, as people like Daniel are the ones you really needed to watch…closely! After Chingford they moved to the beautiful neighbourhood of Buckhurst Hill in Ardmore Lane, and we used to get up to all kinds of unsupervised mischief. We were just fifteen to twenty minutes away from the prying eyes of the older kids and staff from 3 The Ridgeway but it was all the time and space we needed. Here are some of the less dangerous things we got up to.

## Catamarans

Not the sailing craft. I'm talking about two skateboards parallel to each other, me sitting on one board he sitting on the other, our feet straddling both with each other's feet either side of us. It was called a catamaran in skateboard jargon. Daniel usually had the faster skateboard, which was typical, as he always had to have the best. His house was at the bottom of this hilly street which had a few blind hairpins thrown in for good measure, plus the dangerous undulations of the road itself, including large stormwater drain inlets. As we'd set off from the top of the steep hill we'd narrowly miss parked cars on either side. Cars coming up the hill would beep and their drivers shout at us. But we didn't care. Well, actually I was frightened, but Daniel seemed to show no fear, so neither would I! We'd really pick up speed; negotiate the hairpins and the stormwater drains then fall, tumble or worse, somehow avoiding parked cars and serious injury. We'd laugh, lick our wounds, walk back up to the top of Ardmore Lane and go again, seemingly undeterred by the succession of near misses which had just befallen us. Sometimes we'd also involve his younger brother Simon in our shenanigans.

### Over 100 miles an hour!

There were so many firsts with Daniel. I remember his dad, who could be easily convinced to be equally fun, had a succession of sports cars over the years. It was in his Volkswagen Scirocco which was the first time I'd been in a car and clocked over 100 miles per hour, at an abandoned airstrip not far from Buckhurst Hill. We were chased off by security. Staying with the car theme, years later Daniel would be at the helm for my first car accident. The superfast, agile Renault 5 GT Turbo was quite a car by all accounts. Four people, girls and guys, squeezed inside, and I was in the rear passenger seat. We were travelling at speed, entering a semi-densely packed area, when the car went into a skid and started spinning. Out of control, heading towards parked cars, not a great feeling I can tell you. Whether we hit parked cars or missed most of them I can't confirm as it happened so fast. What I do remember after the car finally came to a stop was a passer-by shouting to get out of the car as it was about to blow up.

## Night guy, stealth mode

I was close to being legal age but back then I was tall and was never asked for my ID, and North Chingford had some of the best bars in the area. In these hunting grounds I bore witness to the most phenomenal, stunning, girl pick-up machine I think I'd ever seen. Daniel was on fire! Whilst his self-esteem was reaching dizzying heights in the stratosphere, mine were plummeting into subterranean tunnels. How could I compete with this guy! Yep I was in awe. This continued for years it felt like, when out of the blue, as we were heading back to one of the places Daniel said we might see that girl again who said 'Who's that handsome guy?' – the penny didn't drop until much later that he was referring to me! Someone out there of the opposite species, referred to me as handsome. This was a turning point!

I don't think I ever saw the girl he mentioned, or perhaps Daniel with all his perceptive wisdom could have made it up. I didn't ask nor wanted to know the answer. A girl thought that of me. Self-esteem hit for a home run. Here's the thing, it doesn't matter when, where, what or how, it's about what you trick yourself into thinking about yourself that makes the difference. Confidence is attractive no matter how the person looks! Decades later I found Italian women to be some of the sexist on the planet because of this very same outlook – they interact with confidence. Weeks after that comment I had more success, more courage with women romantically than ever before. The power of a healthy mindset.

## Nics, America and the Tongariro Crossing

Nicky was a stunning, tall blonde with a great body, who didn't take herself too seriously. She was funny with a wicked sense of wit, quick thinking, super creative and we got along right away. So much so we moved in to share house with three other girls in Southampton. She was studying Art at Southampton University and I was studying Leisure Studies (water based), the first course of its kind in Warsash on River Hamble at the Maritime Institute, a few miles away.

After two years of study and a lot of laughs we made the decision to go travelling – actually Nics made that decision for herself and I had the good sense to postpone whatever I was planning and join her, which thankfully she agreed to. I was twenty years of age.

We took driveaway cars through the USA including Hawaii, and sold green recycling policy door to door in Seattle. What are driveaway cars I hear you ask? The USA is vast. When locals want to go on vacation or holidays they want to have their car where they are going but don't want to drive there. They hand their car over to a driveaway agency which employs foreign drivers (usually travellers) to drive their car to that destination, where the owner then collects their car from the nearest driveaway agency – presumably they flew instead.

It's a win-win. The traveller acquires a vehicle free of charge (except fuel) to travel and the owner can drive their car on their vacation without having to drive it there in the first place. There is usually a limitation on the number of extra kilometres you can take to reach the destination. Also, you are not insured to travel at night, given that plenty of accidents occur at night time as cattle and livestock wander across the road in many parts of the USA. So naturally we always did hundreds of kilometres over the limit and drove at night so we could see more during the day! We drove our first car from Chicago to Seattle. The second, Seattle to San Diego and third San Diego to Albuquerque New Mexico. Anytime we returned a car we would put on the charm, ensuring we'd milk the English accent, which our American counterparts absolutely loved and thought was 'cute'. At that time it was the ace up our sleeves. The only question we were ever asked was 'did she drive well'. We saw so much, did so much – any National Park, whether close to our route or not, we saw. I loved that trip and the time we spent – it was amazing!

Next stop after Hawaii was New Zealand. We talked our way into managing a hostel in Taupo (we had no experience) and were picked up hitchhiking by the son of the president of New Zealand's most powerful tribe, who hooked us up all over the North Island with other members of their extended family to stay with. We drove both North and South Islands respectively, a once in a lifetime experience! But it was a day walk called the

Tongariro Crossing which would for me personally be a life-changing experience because of how close Nicky and I came to a probable death. This track is a lot safer now but a few weeks before we did it two German tourists died from exposure.

## Mounts Ngauruhoe, Ruapehu and Tongariro

In Taupo there are three mountains, Mount Ngauruhoe, Mount Ruapehu and Mount Tongariro. Like many great walks you can do daytrips, small walks or stay overnight at a succession of little, basic huts littered all over the trail. We decided to do the long day walk. We arrived early with very basic supplies – emphasis on 'basic', that is, we were not prepared for alpine conditions so were grossly underprepared. The hike would take you up Mount Ngauruhoe, across the plateau past Mount Ruapehu towards the Ketetahi Hut and down Mount Tongariro. As I said, it was a full day's walk. We had basic maps and a compass and little to no wet weather or cold weather clothing, with no real contingency for blizzards or a protracted stay on the plateau.

With beautiful weather expected and the sun on our backs we started up Ngauruhoe and onto the plateau, which probably took some hours to do. Here's what came next.

Alpine conditions change remarkably quickly but neither of us had a lot of experience. We were walking on the plateau towards the Ketetahi Hut. The sun was beautiful, visibility clear for hundreds of metres. We noticed some clouds far off on the horizon but didn't pay them any attention. The scene is beautiful, typical of an alpine environment in New Zealand, comprising beautiful bush, trees, rocks, the occasional lake, vivid colours surrounded by three large, snow-capped mountains. Some parts of the walk you can see off the plateau towards the rest of New Zealand below and it really is stunning. Literally within thirty minutes or less we went from walking, talking, having fun to rapidly deteriorating conditions. It was now overcast and beginning to snow, we could see a sort of hazy weather pattern approaching rapidly and we stopped and put on whatever other clothes we had as it was getting cold. We considered turning back but agreed we were too far in to turn back. The hut couldn't be that far away. It was around then we began to realise that we hadn't seen anyone else for hours. We kept pushing ahead, sort of confident of the direction that we were going as we stopped to check the map. We are optimistic people so we were keeping it upbeat, laughing and joking around.

## Sometimes things just get worse

The situation was getting worse not better. The hazy weather pattern quickly approaching was actually a blizzard! We were now stuck. Visibility was decreasing rapidly what was as a far as the eye could see was now a matter of metres. We checked our bearings and direction to ensure we were heading for the Ketetahi hut but it was hard to see. I can't speak for Nics, but I was beginning to consider if we really were on track, but I kept it positive as I didn't want to scare

Nics (not that she's the type to be easily scared anyway). In my mind I repeatedly took stock of our situation; we hadn't seen anyone for hours, the signage on the walk wasn't great, visibility was worsening, now down to mere metres, we were not following any clearly defined path, we were out in the open in a blizzard and we couldn't really hear properly either. Underneath my still chirpy exterior, fear started to enter. My self-talk was beginning to go crazy; I could see how those two German tourists could die here and I didn't want to die. I always feel protected but is there a certain time that you believe you're in trouble, or does death creep up on you?

Not really talking now, perhaps we were both dealing with our self-talk and had stopped putting a brave face on it – we were in trouble and out of our depth. We heard something over the blizzard. I couldn't locate where it was coming from but it was a different sound. I heard it again. My ears tuned to its frequency. There it was again – I thought it was getting closer. I could see maybe 5 metres in front and to the side I was regularly checking that I didn't lose sight of Nics. I could hear that sound more clearly; it was closer now. 'Where are you going?' Huh?! Two climber types appeared, coming from the left down a steep slope. 'Where are you going?' they said in either a German or Slavic tone of voice I think. 'Ketetahi Hut,' we replied. 'You're going the wrong way; we have just come from there! It's that way,' they said, gesturing to a direction more than 90 degrees difference from where we were heading!

They looked well prepared with goggles, crampons, jackets, and proper navigation. And just like that we were saved! We exchanged no more words than that. They went off to wherever they were going and we changed direction to get to where we needed to go.

## Luck, luck and more luck

Let's put this into perspective, we were on plateau, tens of square miles of plateau, visibility was next to nothing, we hadn't seen anyone in hours (even when visibility was good), we were going the wrong way and we were completely unprepared. They came from the Ketetahi Hut that we were supposed to be going to. Finding a needle in a haystack doesn't even come close! We were heading for big trouble as there was no hut in the direction we were going. Yet we somehow found each other.

I don't think Nics or I thought we were going to die, but who does? Did Lee think another day playing pool was going to end the way it did. Did beautiful Jackie think that was the last time she was going to ride pillion on Pete's, or anyone's bike, for that matter? That experience stayed with me for years – I think if anything it reinforced the mindset of living your life fully, and of course not being ridiculously unprepared.

## Bella time

How can I sum up seventeen plus years of relationship in a single chapter? From my late twenties onwards I was probably exposed to the most sustained period of personal growth and development yet.

We met in a yoga or meditation retreat put on by Shanti Mandir in Sydney in the presence of Mahamandaleshwar, at that time, Nityananda, the chosen successor to Baba Muktananda, who it is said was an enlightened meditation master (classical Indian). During that relationship we also met the divine mother and some of the most well-known personal development gurus on the planet such as Michael Domeyko Rowland, Dr Wayne Dyer, Bob Proctor, Louise Hay and Jerry and Esther Hicks. Many of these we met through a good friend at the time, Leon Nacson of Hay House, who also toured most of these names and always had us front and centre whenever they came – he really was so generous with us and many others. During that relationship I was exposed to the work of financial gurus like Robert Kiyosaki, Brian Tracy, Buckminster Fuller, Jack Canfield, Zig Ziglar; relational gurus, Dr John De Martini, Akash, Nick Kovacs and the Neurolink modality, body gurus such as the wonderful chiropractor Fiona Norman and food gurus like Don Tolman and the search for ancient grains.

Bella used her body as a guinea pig, a training ground where she practised what she preached, many times to my discontent as some of her views challenged my socks off and I was so uncomfortable watching her seemingly crucifying her body and sometimes her mind. Ultimately, that was my issue and I made it hers, which was unfair of me. She was so advanced with diet, grains, ways of being, the whole Zeitgeist that in hindsight I would have to concede she was before her time, a pioneer of sorts. The mainstream world has now embraced many of things she was questioned about following. Through herself and her highly developed spiritually aware mum Krystyna (and stepfather Richard), a reflexologist and so much more, she was also instrumental in bringing out Est, the forerunner to the Landmark Forum, arguably one of the most powerful, well-priced personal development/human potential courses of its kind on the planet.

The effect of sugar in the diet, vaccines, the body's homeostatic mechanisms, the whole paleo way, gluten-free movement, dairy free, vegan – she was light years ahead as she found and engaged some of the most enlightened teachers in those areas on planet earth; like David Wolfe, years before the mainstream knew who he was. She went much further than this but would definitely be beyond the scope of a book like this one.

So what was the turning point here? Well there were too many to mention, some of which I'll pick up upon in the final part of this book, the five keys. What I will highlight for now is the power of understanding that your life, no matter how great or not, is the sum total of the experiences, thoughts and ideas that occupy your mind most, that is, you become what you think about most. You can change the way your life works by how you think. This changed my life and wreaks havoc on me and my life whenever I go away from it, or don't employ and pass on what I have learnt!

## Looking good versus authenticity

One of the breakthroughs I received from the doing The Landmark Forum (there were many) was the concept of 'looking good' versus 'authenticity' – the quality of being real or true. Telling the truth instead of being evasive because you want to cover up the truth.

Let me expand upon this, how many times are you feeling sub par (or not at your best) when someone asks you, 'How are you doing?' You immediately respond 'great' or' good' when you know that is untrue. How about when your life isn't going that great, you're in a really tough spot and things really aren't going your way? When asked, 'How are things going?' Instead of telling the truth by saying, 'I'm going through a really tough spot at the moment and I don't know if I'm going to make it to the other side and that actually scares me as I have a family to support,' what is the response that comes out of your mouth? 'Good thanks.'

This condition of not wanting to be authentic, vulnerable or tell the truth has some potentially very damaging repercussions. For many years growing up where I did, the sign of having 'made it' was signified or summed up in owning a BMW car. I have nothing against BMW, nor having the money to legitimately purchase one if within your true financial capability. Over the years I bought two (not at the same time). If I was being honest or authentic with myself, the second one I could not afford. If I was being authentic with myself, I bought it because my self-esteem was lower than I was prepared to admit and

I needed that car, a thing, to tell me and the world that 'I made it'. In actuality I didn't need the car to tell me this. Years later myself and my family felt the true financial repercussions of my poor decision-making, borne out of the fact I wasn't being authentic with myself about 'why' I bought that car. Prior to that I had three $10,000 plus credit-card debts over a twelve-year period, once again care of an inability to be honest and authentic with myself because I wanted to 'look good' or present the face to the world of a successful man. What a crock! Looking good is currently costing Australia the unenviable title of largest personal debt per capita in THE WORLD! Living beyond your means, spending more than you earn. I'd bet looking good, keeping up with the Joneses, immediate gratification as opposed to 'delayed' gratification is beneath it, and I am guilty as charged – but I needed to learn my lesson and make the change..

# CHAPTER 13

# MAN IN THE MIRROR (NO, NOT MICHAEL JACKSON!)

### Looks are everything?

I was never comfortable with how I looked physically from the get go, and like everything else, the more you focus on what you perceive to be lacking the more lack you see so the uglier I became in my eyes. It came to a head in my very early teens where I had already developed a public persona or identity. I was well liked at school, had a great bunch of friends, and was extremely good at sport, which endeared me even further to that community. According to my personal confidential file reviews, I was achieving in leaps and bounds and they were all very proud of me. In the midst of having all of this going for me publicly, I never felt so alone personally. I never shared this with anyone really – what could they do? They were not able to change my physical appearance.

What I didn't fully appreciate at the time was that my desire to be seen, to matter, to make a difference, to excel was the same thing holding me prisoner at home. I would take to the solace of my room for what seemed like hours at a time armed with a mirror. I'd put the mirror up to my face and study what I would change about my face. My nose was too broad, my lips too big, my face too long and thin. I would practise reining in my bottom lip utilising the muscles in the lower half of my jaw nearest the lip. I would put my tongue under my top lip and gently push. This would narrow my nose and nostrils but unfortunately also narrow my face still further, and in silhouette would look like the profile of a dog. Whilst on my profile, the years of sucking my fingers and resting my hand on my jaw had effectively pulled my whole jaw down so it wasn't square like my sister's and younger brother's. When it came to dentistry, I had no rest there either from the eye of criticism; my teeth were, in short, bad! To make matters worse my smile was flawed and the teeth of my lower and upper jaws didn't meet, even when my jaws were shut together…they still don't. All of this we can finish off nicely with a pointed head – which in an ancient tribe in Africa would bestow some kind of great honour. But here on planet Earth, in the place I lived, it was just another thing that counted against me in the game of life. Then came the real cause of my challenge, 'If I'm not good looking, I'm not going to have friends and make it in this life.'

## White man in a black man's skin

Even though I lived in a children's home that had a black majority, the place where I spent the longest time was at school where 99 per cent of the population was white! So unimaginably to anyone who knows me, let alone who can see me, I was convinced that I was white. All my standards and views about the world came through the veil of a Caucasian viewpoint: beauty, look, feel, my future partner, kids and so on. Part of the source of my pain came from here. When playing sport and having that outstanding success I was in the moment, in the zone. Thoughts of skin tone, features and the like were not part of my thought processes. But away from being caught up in the moment playing sport, my mind had time to ponder on this.

This mindset continued even after I became a model and had some great successes modelling with some of the best in the world, who were in the same agency. Riccardo Gay Model Management in Milan represented the supermodels such as Naomi Campbell, Linda Evangelista, Eva Herzigová, Christy Turlington and Marcus Schenkenberg. But that wasn't the thing that gave me acceptance. Try being in a room with a bunch of models – you'd be so surprised about how negative their self-image is, and these are some of the most incredible-looking humans on the planet!

### Positive self-image strikes back!

For the hours, days and years I suffered in silence unbeknownst to anyone, the secret to overcoming it started with something tiny. By the way, that's not to say I believe I'm a super-stunning guy who's God's gift to women, but it did make me feel comfortable in my own skin.

One of those early days, as I sat there criticising and self-loathing, I stumbled upon meditation – the ability to focus on something for an extended period of time. Though at first it was a negative focus on lack, on what I didn't have. Later, when I quietened my mind, I was able to hear other voices in my head instead of the inner critic. Over the years I've spoken to many people about this and the answer has been the same more often than not – it's that supportive inner voice you're looking to seek out, the one that reminds you you are not above or beneath anyone and you have the right to have high self-esteem, be happy and successful. Not the one pushing you into competition with others and self-loathing. I remember the first time I heard this voice, which said the most bizarre thing as I sat there weeping on my bed, 'Just look after your skin!'

I'm not sure whether it was out of shock or just that the fact that for the first time I felt good about something to do with myself, and it was such a supportive, comfortable, warm voice – like my best friend that I didn't know I had. Little did I know this was the start of something which would change my life. I'll go into more details on this in the final section of this book called the five keys!

### Playing basketball for England?

Between the ages of thirteen and fourteen I remember thinking that it was time for me to decide on which sport I could excel in. Any sport with a moving ball (except cricket) I had a natural aptitude for, that hand–eye, ball coordination. I loved sport; it gave me the ability to be who I wanted to be. It wasn't based on colour, birthright or how much money you had. It was based on skill, perseverance, discipline, willpower and mindset. Growing up at 3 The

Ridgeway, it felt like I had to fight for almost everything. The things that happened to me, and those around me such as Lee and Jackie, filled me with more discipline, more drive to make it. I was intensely competitive with sport and I hated losing – even when it was just for fun!

I became more focused; I still played and excelled in the other sports but basketball became more important. At school, I would practise during break times, lunchtimes, after school. I started to research which teams acted as feeder teams to the South England Team Trials. It just so happened I was in a great spot with East London Royals. I trained with them, practised with them, played games with them. I wasn't one of the best players but I probably was one of the people who worked the hardest. I would ask the coach what I could do to improve, what did I need to do to get better. I would attend basketball skills clinics during the summer school holiday break. I got along with all the squad; I've always had the ability to get along with people of whatever background. I became an expert in disarming people, mentally and emotionally, so they didn't feel threatened by me. Ultimately basketball is a game where an individual can have a huge bearing on the game but a well-oiled team will mostly beat an individual. So I focused on being a team player.

Sometime later I think I was rewarded for all this effort with a trial for the South East England team, which I managed to ace – I passed that test. There were more basketball clinics, but where I struggled the most was learning the plays. A play is a set offence or defence to combat different situations. On the court at any one point in time there are five players on each team. Each player is given a number, which related to their role in the team. Number 1 is called a point guard, or on-court leader. They are usually the shortest, most explosive, great passers of the ball who can, dribble, penetrate the defence by driving to the basket with the ability to read the game and react appropriately. Number 2 is a bit taller and has the role of 'shooting' guard. They can also handle the ball, but are great shooters. Number 3 is the swingman, or a small forward. He can drive, pass, shoot and handle the ball. Number 4 is the forward. The second tallest player in general plays close to the basket, where they can rebound, take the ball and attack the basket. Number 5 is the centre and usually the tallest on court. Again, like the number 4, they play 'inside', or very close to the basket, with penetration, rebounding and scoring from inside the key.

On offence and defence each of these players have a specified position on the court. Offence for example, is the process by which your team, utilising the players on court, is able to create as many scoring opportunities as possible. The role of the defence is to stop them scoring or make it extremely difficult to do so. Different plays (plan to score) involve different players. One play may be created for the number 4 or 5 man to get an easy score close to the basket. Another play may aim to free up the number 1, 2 or 3 for a high percentage outside shot, and so on. I was athletic enough to play number 2, 3 or 4. In short, I had to learn the plays for each one! I persevered after numerous times being caught out, substituted or benched! Our coach didn't take well to the players on court not knowing their plays and those of their teammates.

I earned the right to trial for the full England squad (which would be then whittled down in number to create the England team). I don't know if many people thought that I would make the squad. My defence was pretty solid and if anything I was becoming more of a defensive specialist. My arm and hand reach were long enough to guard (or defend) players far taller than me, typically the number 4 and 5 men. Yet I was just quick enough to guard the speedier number 2 and number 3, with the advantage that I could shut them out of the game by my long arms and hands in the passing lane, so I was able to anticipate, steal or intercept the ball (with amazing regularity). I would learn if my back was ever to the ball to look into the eyes of my opponent and see when the ball was coming by reading him, his body language and his hands! I think this was the reason not only why I made it into the squad but also survived 'the cut' to make it into the England under-15 team. I was an average shooter, I could dribble the ball well enough, but I was a team player, who would hustle, stifle and make it really difficult for the player I was marking to even acquire the ball. If they did I was able to spoil their game and make it really difficult for them to score. I wasn't a regular starting-five player (who commenced the game), probably first, second or third substitute depending on the flow of the game. We played throughout the UK and in Europe and I had an amazing experience which I'll never forget. But it was the perseverance, work ethic, team player-bonding and visualisation (dealt with in the five keys chapter) that got me over the line. I think I was probably one of first people from a children's home to achieve this (I also received a sponsorship from adidas) and later had the opportunity to go to American College on a basketball scholarship.

# PART 4
# SUCCESS AT LAST

# CHAPTER 14

# GOOD GOD BLESS AMERICA!

This part of the book marks some of the most prolific times in my life, where I learnt the most by failing some of the time but also having some amazing successes. Out of one decision all of this came into being so I really want to thank, firstly, Nics for having the greatest idea of travelling around the world for a year and, secondly, myself for swallowing my 'ego' of believing that I had all my life worked out and actually asking Nics if I could come too. This all occurred at the end of Southampton University for Nics and the Warsash Campus – The Maritime Institute for me, respectively. We worked for between six months to a year to raise money however we could – I was a pushbike courier in London for a company called Metro. Armed with our outgoing personalities, accents, openness, willingness to put ourselves out there – potentially in harm's way – with a positive mindset and both at the tender age of twenty/twenty-one, during spring/summer in the Northern Hemisphere of 1992 we embarked upon the trip of a lifetime backpacking.

# CHAPTER 14

First on our around-the-world ticket was the United States of America. It seemed that wherever you would travel in the world back then, it was really easy to point out the epitome of the 'typical' American tourist – often brash, proud, over-confident – teetering on the brink of being insensitive with the inspired belief that they were from the best country on earth. Having spent some months travelling around there I could really understand how mistaken I was and why that country in many ways is really very special. As you will see below the United States of America really is a treasure chest where, geology meets geography and topography rolled into one. For instance if you want to ski, the Rocky Mountains arguably offer some of the best skiing on the planet. Water/desert islands look no further than Hawaii, Maui (just to start with). If you would like to experience the energy of a city that never sleeps, New York. Would you like desert, salt flats, jungle, river, delta and some of the most highly prized national parks in the world? The United States of America does have it all.

Nics and I landed in New York and spent some days there living in downtown New York, though we took in the typical tourist sights – Empire State building, Manhattan, Twin Towers, Statue of Liberty and so on. I was amazed by the enormity of it all, the non-stop go-go-go energy night and day which pervaded everything. However, most of all it was the 'CAN DO' attitude which was most on display in the architecture, the restaurants, the bars, the people, their attitude! I didn't find quite the same attitude when I played some pick-up basketball games with some street kids somewhere up near Harlem – all was going great until I was asked about money, my life in London and what we were doing now. I think to them, we were very wealthy and privileged and it was time for me to go. We visited Washington the city of monuments and galleries and later partied in Georgetown courtesy of a good friend Daniel hooking us up with some of his friends, as he studied there.

## Driveaway car number one:
## Chicago to Seattle

As I mentioned before, we headed on up to Chicago, stayed in New England and up to Montreal via Niagara Falls.

There really is something about seeing one of the wonders of the world and Niagara Falls took my breath away. It was the enormity of it, the ferocious power of water cascading hundreds of feet to the plunge pool below, the spray you felt from hundreds of metres away. We stayed with a friend of a friend whilst in Quebec, a little town by the name of Lachine. Fierce, fiery and French, we were in the land of the French Canadians and had stumbled upon the fight for independence of Quebec from the rest of Canada. Back down to Chicago we took our first driveaway* car, a Toyota Celica I think, from a company called Autodriveway, one of the biggest in the US. We went from Chicago to Seattle, basically 3000 plus kilometres from east to west and from memory were given five days to do it. We drove past or through dozens of national forests, monuments, recreation parks, wild and scenic rivers and over 25 million acres of wilderness, mountains, lakes, rivers and canyons. Including but not limited to the Great Mall Of America, Montana, Wyoming, Spokane, South Dakota, Badlands, Yellowstone, Grand Tetons, Devil's Tower National Landmark, Glacier National Park, Custer National Park – Battle of The Little Bighorn and Wounded Knee and The Black Hills (cowboys and Indians again!). I even remember seeing signs for Nebraska. We would drive at night (when we were not supposed to nor insured to) and during the day would dogleg on every possible occasion to see a sight of special interest along the way. In the mornings, after driving all night we would find a McDonald's or some other fast food joint and freshen up using the sink or shower available, that way we saved on time and the expense of accommodation. One drove one slept. I can't tell you the number of times we narrowly avoided roadkill or wild animals at night. On one occasion whilst Nics was asleep, I was so tired I entered a freeway going the wrong the way! I was thankful to have seen one of those HUGE maxi signs with words to the effect of 'You Are Going The Wrong Way'. Up until that time I remember very judgementally commenting on what was the need for having a sign such as that! When we reached Seattle to deliver the car to the driveaway agency we received our deposit without issue, even though we were many hundreds of kilometres over our quota. But we had the spirit of America within us – the 'can do' spirit – we flirted, we used our 'cute' accent and our intuition to the highest extent possible to ensure they wouldn't ask the question nor look at the speedometer to see how many kilometres we had actually travelled. At least before we had our deposit back!

## Driveaway car number two:
## Seattle to San Diego

After a stint in Seattle selling recycling policy door to door in attempt to keep ourselves as liquid as possible, we repeated the process two more times. The second car, a compact, we were to take from Seattle to San Diego, close to the Mexican border, a drive of some 2000 plus kilometres down the beautiful western coastline of the US. We took in the conurbations of Portland, Bakersfield, Sacramento, San Francisco, San Jose, Las Vega and Los Angeles. Once again there were stunning national parks, chance meeting with locals, a can-do attitude with a positive mind frame, along with the gift of the gab – especially when it came time to deliver the car and receive our deposit whilst trying to distract whoever was on a reception from even thinking about looking at the speedometer!

San Francisco was everything we had assumed and far too much to go into here. It really is one of the most eclectic cities we saw in the US, home to hipsters, techies, immigrants, fine art, street art and one of the most established gay scenes probably on the planet. The Golden Gate Bridge, Alcatraz, Haight Ashbury, we immersed ourselves in as much as we could for the very limited time we had there before moving on to San Diego. But I would say that if I learnt anything from our short time in San Francisco, it was that, as with our friend in Lachine, Quebec, there was a fierce commitment to being who you are, and unapologetically so. This was especially evident in the gay scene, from the shop and restaurant ownership to some of the extremely talented artists on the street.

From a personal standpoint our final driveaway car, from San Diego to Albuquerque, New Mexico, was in many ways one of the most interesting journeys and highlighted the power of, above all things, colours!

# CHAPTER 15

# NEW ZEALAND, THE KINDNESS OF MAN AND A MINIBUS

If America was about creating, harnessing and unleashing a can-do attitude, New Zealand was about the kindness of man and opportunity!

In many ways New Zealanders and Jamaicans have a kindred connection, which I have only recently considered. Both had an indigenous route long before 'civilisation' reached them. Both were able – through struggle, willpower, violence and an insatiable desire for independence – to manage to carve out a treaty of some description in return for rights, land and ultimately a way to coexist, such as the First Maroon Treaty* and the Treaty of Waitangi** for the Jamaicans and Maori respectively.

In the North Island Nics and I were outside the Waipoua Forest after seeing Tane Mahuta, the oldest kauri tree in New Zealand and perhaps the world (and one of the most famous). Darkness was coming and we were hours away from the nearest town. Quite frankly the idea of hitchhiking and backpacking, carrying heavy backpacks and walking a lot, was beginning to lose its lustre for me. Having said that, hitchhiking was the best way to get around New Zealand if you had limited or no budget! We noticed there were no cars in either direction for some time, there was no Uber back then, but beautiful rolling green fields with sheep on the other hand, were in plentiful supply. I think in the back of my mind I was beginning to entertain the thought of sleeping in a field of sheep. I fought that thought away with another in its place 'something good will come along', and kept that in the forefront of my mind.

At some stage we probably didn't notice a minibus moving 'not too quickly' (and that's an understatement) was approaching us from the direction of the Waipou Forest, heading in the direction we wanted to go! This was our last chance. Out went the thumbs. The minibus stopped and let us in. Inside was full. We had stumbled on a bunch of students shooting a documentary. There have been so many lucky coincidences that have followed me for what seems like my whole life; a kind of guiding hand pushing me in the appropriate direction, or pulling me toward another direction if I needed to learn a lesson. This synchronicity reminds me of being 'in the zone'. In basketball it's when the whole game slows down in a way and you can clearly see what needs to be done and that's precisely what you do; whether that's passing, shooting or driving to the hoop – you just know! And it turned out that in that minibus were a film crew from the Ngapuhi tribe.

## Ngapuhi tribe

Ngapuhi is the largest tribe in New Zealand and in that minibus was Lloyd Latimer, son of the president of the Ngapuhi tribe. Not only were we saved but we had inadvertently hopped into the minibus of one of the most influential people in the North Island. Lloyd himself was also a beautiful, soulful and compassionate human being. We stayed with him that night and he informed us as that as we made our way down the North Island he'd organise some friends and family to look after us, which we thought was more than enough and really gave it no second thought. We had dodged a bullet, or a night sleeping in a field of sheep, after all!

As we said our hearty goodbyes the next day the Maori way, by rubbing noses, we hitchhiked down the North Island to the next the village. We sat down, from memory, near a bus stop, when a sedan appeared and stopped opposite us. One of the Maori occupants rolled down the window and enquired 'Are you Rob and Nicky?' In my mind I didn't know what to say or admit to, as I'd already forgotten what Lloyd said the night before. I didn't know who these people were! Then came words to the effect of, 'Lloyd Latimer told us you were coming.' We got in. This repeated itself a few more times on the way down the North Island.

*1738 Maroon Treaty with the British. The purpose of the treaty was fundamentally to find a way to live together, though on separate land within Jamaica. The Maroons operated and controlled their lands within Jamaica whilst the British operated and controlled their own.

** The Treaty of Waitangi (Te Tiriti o Waitangi) is an important agreement that was signed by representatives of the British Crown and Maori in 1840. The purpose of the treaty was to enable the British settlers and the Maori people to live together in New Zealand under a common set of laws or agreements.

## Taupo, slap bang in the middle of the North Island

A total stranger had extended his hand out to us and looked after us throughout the North Island and we bonded and came to know another culture way of life and experienced insights the likes of which wouldn't have come our way had we not reached out just a bit further than most were prepared to. That experience as you can imagine set the tone for the rest of our stay in New Zealand. There were so many firsts there: from bathing in sulphur hot springs in Rotorua, completing the Tongariro Alpine Crossing, bungy jumping, the Bay Of Islands and Huka Falls. We hired a four-wheel drive and drove the South Island, experiencing some of the most stunning scenery I have ever seen, including Fox Glacier, the Milford Track, Wanaka and driving over Arthur's Pass. In the North Island, in Taupo we actually ran a backpackers' hostel for a short time. We had the spirit of adventure in us and just kept putting ourselves out there and trying new things. I think Nics may have seen the advert somewhere and we decided to respond and basically talked our way in to doing something neither of us had ever done, nor were qualified to do. That can-do attitude struck again. What I remember about our time at Burke's Backpackers was changing beds, washing, telephone operations, meeting new people from different parts of the world from all walks of life and nursing hangovers after spending time in the hot tub drinking – a lethal combination!

# CHAPTER 16

# THE LIGHT OF SYDNEY!

**W**e reached Sydney, broke, with the need to work and find an income source. I'm not sure how we heard of the now-closed Pink House in Barncleuth Square, Kings Cross – probably Nics and her *Lonely Planet* guide – but it was an inspired move. As described on the website, the Pink House was:

> …an historic Victorian mansion built in 1848, with leafy gardens and sunny courtyards, offering a clean, quiet, relaxed and safe home away from home. The Pink House offers a friendly atmosphere, a great social life and provides a perfect base for travellers in Sydney…the Pink House has long been a welcome oasis for travellers from all over the world. Our friendly and helpful staff can assist with anything from travel arrangements to looking for work.

What made the Pink House different in 1992 was its job opportunities. Whether officially sanctioned by the Pink House or whether part of the space was subleased I can't be sure, however we made up dry flower bundles and got paid a nominal amount (still very low – but better than nothing!).

One week later I decided to take the dried flower bundles on the road, from memory, out to the western suburbs of Sydney, which back in those days was considered rough, and sell the flowers door to door. Part of the proceeds went to charity, but you could earn infinitely more.

## Flower power

I remember days of selling absolutely no dried flower bundles and being miserable. I found tens of dozens of ways to have a door slammed in my face. It was not pleasant. Occasionally, someone would open the door and be happy to listen, by which time I was in such a rush to get through my scripted dialogue that I would push the potential sale away! I think it all changed, perhaps weeks later, when I found that cheeky can-do attitude that had reared its head in the USA months prior. Almost immediately it felt like it began to click! No longer did I even bother to get on the train. I sold all the flowers, probably illegally, at Kings Cross train station whilst walking up and down the escalators. I targeted single women or older women who looked like they would appreciate the attention. I sold so many I would go back to the Pink House for repeat orders. The gift of the gab was coming alive and people seemed to really like it. I don't think they bought the flowers because they wanted flowers but as an exchange for making them feel better. They purchased emotionally. I was learning something!

## Claire Croxon

Claire Croxon was a soulful girl who I have known since I was three years old. She was like my sister and always one of my closest friends until the teenage years when we lost regular contact. Claire was tall, a tad gangly, and some would say a little socially awkward (that wasn't my opinion). In any case, I remember the girls back in secondary at school who were small minded, conniving, rude, pretentious and just a little bit bitchy. These were more often than not the pretty girls who found make-up early and probably smoked. They traded their looks for power and milked it for all it was worth. Claire was never one of those girls. I don't remember who said it but we become a reflection on the outside of who we really are inside. At sixth form (around seventeen years of age) I saw the pretty girls with an ugly heart or a genuine disrespect for people become unattractive and the girls who had a beautiful soul became gorgeous, physically speaking, whilst retaining that beautiful soul. This is what happened to Claire. During the years that I didn't see her, she had become a very successful international model. So you could imagine my surprise when on the other side of the world whilst crossing Darlinghurst Road in front of Tatler (for those who know Sydney) I bumped right into her! The next thing that happened was another one of those instances that was to change my life forever with just five words. After the chit-chat Claire said, 'You could probably work here'!

What she meant was, as a model I could probably work in Sydney, and we did a test together (photographs with a professional photographer). One of the agencies I went to was Ursula's or Chic Model Management.

## Chic Model Management

Ursula Hufnagl was a beautiful, tough, strong woman with a discerning eye. She found Kate Fischer, guiding her to become one of the most successful and recognised Australian models and actress around the world, and many more like her. She was fierce, but somehow from the beginning I got along naturally with her and Dominic, her softly spoken, handsome husband who had a sexy French-sounding accent and a truly wicked sense of humour.

Ursula was straight with me from the beginning – she said there wasn't a lot of work for your look, but you will get commercials, the occasional acting job, catwalk and editorial. That's exactly what I got! I went on castings (job interviews for models) and secured some great jobs. There was a Gatorade commercial and a lead role as Chasen in a short film called *Shotgunning*, directed by filmmaker Sean Byrne and shot by the amazing Denson Baker (now an award winning director of photography). It was a story about a sprinter and doping. There was also an editorial in *Juice Magazine* shot by Ben Watts (brother of the famous actress Naomi Watts); I shot Gianni Versace for fashion boutique Five Way Fusion, a number of body editorial shoots by Garth Boyd, and others featured in award-winning magazines such as *Attitude*. I shot with the famous Brett M Cochrane who devised and shot the book *Catherine: Intimate Portrait of a Champion*, a beautiful book about Olympian Cathy Freeman. These are just the jobs that come to mind. But what modelling really gave me was the key to opening up Sydney.

A very proud moment for me after making the England under-15 basketball team. Couldn't wipe the smile off my face from here on in! I'm number 10 (on the right-hand side).

A bird's eye view from the top of the mountain of the spectacle that is the Byblos club in Misano Adriatico, Riccione, Italy.

A body shot of me for the award-winning Attitude magazine shot by Andreas Bitesnich in Sydney.

Tom Corbett shot this one of me (in a mirror) for a story in Juice magazine, Sydney.

### ROBERT IAN BONNICK

A great body shot from Robin Sellick, in Sydney.

Another favourite headshot in Sydney wearing 'that' bright pink shirt which Genna (of G & S fame) made for me many moons ago in Sydney.

# ROBERT IAN BONNICK

## MANIQUE
### MEN
Tel: 0171-610 2302 / Fax: 0171-610 0049

First Floor, 12 Rickett Street, London SW6 1RU

Height 6'2" Suit 44L Collar 16 Chest 44 Waist 32-33 Inseam 34 Shoes 12 Hair Black Eyes Brown
Hauteur 1.88 Confection 54-56 Cou 40 Poitrine 112 Taille 81-84 Pant. Int. 86 Chaussures 46 Cheveux Noir Yeux Bruns

Bottom right: Shot by Andrew Shaylor in London – 1990's.

One of my favourite headshots, shot in London, which formed the front of my composite card when I was with Manique model agency in London.

# ROBERT IAN BONNICK

## MANIQUE
### MEN
Tel: 0171-610 2302 / Fax: 0171-610 0049

First Floor, 12 Rickett Street, London SW6 1RU

Height 6'2" Suit 42L Collar 16 Chest 42 Waist 32-33 Inseam 34 Shoes 12 Hair Black Eyes Brown
Hauteur 1.88 Confection 54-56 Cou 40 Poitrine 112 Taille 81-84 Pant. Int. 86 Chaussures 46 Cheveux Noir Yeux Bruns

Shot in Milan by Franco. The piece of plastic was just lying on the floor minding its own business!

Front cover, shot in Milan by Franco again.

Shot by Franco for Romeo Gigli in Milan.

Shot in Milan for an Italian campaign for Bata wearing Valentino. To this day I haven't worn a suit that felt so good – I wish I could have kept it!

Badly translated as 'Make love with the flavour'. This was my second proudest moment modelling in Milan – the first was doing the same catwalk show as Naomi Campbell. This was a huge billboard campaign in Italy and beyond for Müller yoghurt. Yes, the white dove was sitting on my head!!! It was NOT superimposed.

Franco shot the first photo in Milan. This composite was for the highly prestigious Riccardo Gay – Model Plan in Milan.

## Kickboxing my way to success

Ben Watts, reminded me of a young Marky Mark (Mark Wahlberg); he was handsome, brash and confident with a know-it-all attitude and a massive heart. The kind of guy who would never let down his friends – if he regarded you as one. Through modelling and attending castings I met and got friendly with other models from the same and different agencies and found out about a boxing gym in Paddington where Ben and a few of the models trained. I was still was very fit – sport still played a massive role in my life. I think I loved this form of kickboxing straight away; the spirituality as well as boxing. The teachers, Sir and Roger, were deadly – everyday-looking men (if I can say that) with a power, energy, life force and know-how that was scary. They could tear you apart if they chose to! I met Ben, Tux – a beautiful mixed race male model who was the total package, Dion, Tom and so many more.

Once again synchronistically I found my way into the 'in crew' who ran Sydney's clubs, bars, modelling industry and anything else that was cool. I felt a little out of my depth and when Ben asked me to do a *Reservoir Dogs* type shoot with Tux, Dion and few others I almost fell off the chair I wasn't even sitting on!

## Door bitch, excuse me, 'door host'

Through this crew I ended up working as a host on the door of the most high profile nightspots in Sydney like Soho Bar, Q Bar, Kinselas, Riva, Metropolis and many more. This time would help create all the successes I enjoyed over the next twenty-five years, including one of the ventures I was heavily involved in that was voted number three in the world. But, back to the job of a door host, which cannot be underestimated. The position is instrumental in making the vibe and groove of the night as well as selecting which people go in and which stay outside. The decisions made, in the eyes of the audience, determine who has can have the night of their life or the opposite. The gatekeeper to the most sought after places to go out, which have the prettiest girls, handsome guys and the most influential people in the city.

I was the opposite of a bitch! I did things a little differently, I endeavoured to treat everyone, no matter how they looked, the same, that is, very well. Before going to work each night I would meditate at home in the shower or the bath, bathe myself in a white protective light and ensure I sent any ego present on a holiday. If I had ego on the door whilst dealing with people it could end very badly. Only once in twenty-five years it did!

I was on the front door of Tank nightclub in Sydney one Saturday night. It was an ordinary night by all accounts, capacity inside the venue, a hundred or so people waiting outside. I was standing outside the front door. It was close to midnight and another great night under the belt. Perhaps feeling a bit too full of myself, I didn't even see, let's call him 'Mr A', approaching; a tall, thickly built man of Middle-Eastern origin. I was informing him we were at capacity etcetera and not paying attention or maintaining eye contact. I didn't even see the punch come. I felt the knuckles on the side of my face. I hit the ground headfirst and woke up lying on the inside of the door. I got up and went to the side of the door inside with the security guards. I don't know what we spoke about. Five minutes later I was back on the door like nothing happened! A few months prior a famous Australian cricket player, David Hookes, was punched outside a pub, hit his head on a curb on the way down and later died as a result. My head narrowly missed a curb outside the club. I knew immediately what happened and took full responsibility. I felt embarrassed. I'm always so careful to send my ego on a trip before work – clearly I didn't send it far enough away this time!

**Reprieve**

As it turned out, the guy that hit me was 'connected'. He knew or was part of a side of Sydney to which I didn't belong, which is why the security didn't really respond on the night. But I got the sense that it wasn't the first time I'd overstepped the mark, only this time I was caught out. I learnt something important!

Three weeks later I was standing at the front of the club as usual when a male I didn't recognise approached. I gave my usual chirpy response. He cut to the chase. 'I'm the guy who hit you!' With no hesitation I said, 'I deserved it, I was being a dickhead!' He paused and looked at me dead in the eyes. He wasn't expecting that response. A silent pause ensued. I don't know what was said next but what I said and how it was delivered completely changed the atmosphere between us. I was being completely honest and he felt that. From that moment onwards Mr A had my back. He told me if I ever needed anything at all I only needed to ask. I never did ask for anything but frequently saw him in and about town and he was always extremely civil and showed me respect and kindness, which I always reciprocated and is usually how I treat everyone.

## The key to the city

So as I mentioned above, my role as door host/selector brought out my natural aptitude of bringing people together and inspiring them at the same time. I was happy, wore a natural smile, and would go out of my way to make people comfortable, whether they were coming in or not. Even when saying 'no' I would try to do it in a way that caused as little offence or disrespect as possible. I created and nurtured a family environment where people felt comfortable but would also toe the line if I gave them a certain look, gesture or had a particular discussion. I had an intuitive sense of who to connect with who. Over the years I matchmade more couples, business relationships and friendships than I can remember. At one point in time I had over 20,000 numbers in my phone. I could remember 70–80 per cent of them, including their names, the specific situation and the stories we'd shared. I was in my element. I gave respect and received respect in return. I would in almost all situations use my gift of the gab and intuition to disarm and de-escalate a situation before it became a problem, in the absence of ego. From dealing with a street kid to a drunken lawyer in full possession of the applicable facts of the law, I excelled. My years at 3 The Ridgeway taught me well.

I would be contracted to host the most high-profile functions and events. I met everyone who was anyone in or passing through Sydney at that time: national and international celebrities, fashion designers, event producers, journalists, nightclub owners, promoters, actors, film producers, artists, singers, dancers, PR, agents, managers, sports stars and so much more. Using my gift of the gab* and a can-do attitude I could get along with anyone, regardless of background, age or socioeconomic group. The doors of opportunity were flung open and I ran through them!

*When I use the words 'gift of the gab' what I'm really saying is that I had a sincere deep ability and compassion for seeing the best in all people, regardless of make up or background, and was able to connect with them on that level. I wanted to uplift and inspire them. I still do.

## Boundary Street full of surprises

Around this time I lived in beautifully renovated terrace house in Boundary Street in Paddington. Paddington was a cool and trendy suburb only 10–15 minutes from the city centre. It was a lively, upscale area with busy shops housed within the Victorian terraced buildings along Five Ways and the shopping/eating strip of Oxford Street, which also featured the world famous Paddington Market. The Saturday market opened in 1973 and featured clothing, accessories and home items from local craftspeople, designers, jewellery makers and artists spread over more than 150 unique stalls.

I lived with three housemates, Owen, Clinton and Clem. Owen stood a little less than six feet tall, with a fresh youthful face that belied his true age. He was a keen, talented surfer and skier. A handsome, thoughtful man some years my junior, who would later become an IT creative with his own business, sire a beautiful family and live on acreage with his wife and children, skiing regularly. Clinton's diminutive stature was more than compensated for by possessing those kind, sparkling beautiful blue eyes one could easily get lost in. He was a sharp dresser with an intellect to match, and also another committed and talented surfer. Finally, there was the gorgeous Clementine, the open, gregarious matriarch of the house (I hope she doesn't mind me saying that but she was the eldest and kind of took control of the house in many ways). Once again she possessed the common trait amongst all three of a sharp wit and intellect. She worked in the corporate field, in communications I think. In any case, they were three of the most generous, solid people I have ever met. They were all from the Avalon/Palm Beach area, stunning beachside suburbs of Sydney located north of the CBD.

### Sia, yes Sia!

Into this household came a young, precocious and talented thing with a blonde bob, which years later would become her trademark, that of Sia, the Australian singer-songwriter, record producer and music-video director who captivates the world. For the life of me I can't remember why she came regularly to the house. She knew everyone there and I can't remember who she was particularly close to – perhaps Clem. She was always very polite, sharp a little precocious, with a strong energy and keen sense of humour. From memory, at that time she was singing, acting, and pursuing other creative outlets. Look where she is today. Amazing!

## Meditation and the flickering candle

I had a large room upstairs facing the the leafy, tree-lined street. The significance of this great house in Paddington was many fold but the one that comes to mind as important was for the purposes of meditation. Perhaps it was the peaceful, chilled-out nature of my housemates, or the fact Nics and I had separated; maybe I was in need of some reflective time. Even working at night in the industry I did, during the day I just needed a break. Whatever the reason that HOUSE WAS PERFECT! The only challenge was I didn't know how to meditate!

I remember sitting on the floor at the edge of my bed facing the French doors which looked out onto the balcony, which in turn looked out onto the street. With my back up against the bed I tried to fold up my lanky legs into some kind of lotus position, with my hands resting on my lap. After about two minutes, give or take, my knees felt like buckling. My arms were so long compared to my body it felt like my elbows were resting on the floor. I think I may have lasted five minutes in the position, trying to close my eyes and think of nothing. This was an epic fail! A week later I tried again and faired no better. I just couldn't get it.

**If at first you don't succeed – try again!**

Weeks later I decided to dispense with the lotus position, conceding that my legs were just not made for it. I sat down with my legs out in front of me instead with my back still against the bed. I could now deal with the physical distraction but mentally still couldn't stop my thoughts or quieten my mind. I began to read up on meditation and quickly became fascinated by it: classical Indian, transcendental, open eye, closed eye. It was in this time I read about introducing a candle into the frame. With the addition of a candle my thoughts or focus were directed toward that, not the comings and goings of whatever was happening in my mind. I found by starting first thing in the morning, straight from sleep, that my mind was naturally quieter. I found it easier to sit and stare at this candle in front of me for one or two minutes at first, three or four times per week. Over a series of weeks I became more obsessed. I still really didn't know what I was doing but that didn't seem to matter. On multiple occasions I would try to move the flame with my mind. On a few of these attempts I would swear blind that I was successful and that I moved the flame with my mind. Of course there was no-one there to witness or confirm this, let alone set up consistent test-type conditions. Ultimately, I was in a Victorian terrace house which, even though beautifully renovated, did have gaps underneath doors and numerous draughts all around the place.

Years later I had the good fortune to study with numerous meditation masters, a few of whom were said to be enlightened masters (classical Indian meditation). Then I would truly understand how to meditate and its latent power. Most importantly, it wasn't about stopping your thoughts either. To meditate in its basic form simply meant 'to focus upon', which could be breath, mantra or a candle. Moreover, the practice of mindfulness simply means focusing entirely on the task you are doing right now. To this end I would later realise that all of us have been meditating at some time or another without knowing it. For example, being in the zone when playing a sport, or at work, training, vacuuming, doing housework, watching an engaging play, or documentary – the list is endless. Even in those days of really not knowing anything I acquired some of the benefits of meditating: intuition, mindfulness, paying attention, calmness of mind, clarity, vision… happiness. Only later did I realise that this was the tip of the iceberg. But in many ways Boundary Street is where it started!

**The Sugar Reef**

As I mentioned, I was a door host at some of the coolest joints in town, predominantly in the trendy eastern suburbs and inner city of Sydney in the early 1990s. One such joint was called Soho Bar, located in Victoria Street, Potts Point. It was a hip bar that was part of a larger, not as cool hotel. Friday night was the night where the most beautiful, powerful, eclectic underbelly of Sydney congregated. With a capacity of less than a few hundred this place was packed every Friday and I was one of the guys controlling the door, from early till late, as it usually finished in the early hours. After work, whilst carrying the stress from another successful night, I would make my way, as many key members of the hospitality industry did, to The Sugar Reef.

I wouldn't call it a club, nor a restaurant or bar but a mix of all three, a kind of 'disco bar' Its capacity was a little larger than Soho Bar but still considered small by modern standards. It was owned by the famous Tozzi family from Sicily – four brothers, Antonello, Nicola, Danilo and Roberto, who dominated Sydney during this time. They had the look, the fame, the venues, the money, the pizzazz and the beautiful wives on their arms. This place was jumping! The lowish ceilings added to the vibe; the whole place was a dancefloor and no-one escaped the infectious grooves based in 'house' music, being belted out by the DJ. It opened till very late; or should I say very early! When I left Soho Bar I would swear I would have one drink to wind down then retreat homewards. But each week this would not be the case! When it came to music and dance, if inspired, I had no limits on a dance floor. I would fuse jazz, soul, funk, hip-hop. Remember, I used to copy Gary from the children's home then add my own slant. When I was still at 3 The Ridgeway, I used to dance every Friday night at the disco and I would learn and master new moves and add them to my repertoire. But my biggest advantage was the music itself.

## Guy Chalkley, 'the beatnik'

Between the ages of fourteen and seventeen I had a close friend, Guy Chalkley, the son of Keith Chalkley, a musician who played on the road with many of the great jazz legends of the bebop era such as Dizzy Gillespie. Guy was a super cool beatnik who wouldn't be out of place in a Jack Kerouac novel. This guy (pardon the pun) oozed 'cool' from the way he spoke (slow and steady with colour in his voice) to the way he walked (slow, steady and deliberate). He had swag. A few times a week after school we would go back his house and listen to jazz. A small room, not more than five square metres, was wall to wall in vinyl. But not just any vinyl, most of it was rare vinyl from his father's collection. He taught me, utilising jazz as the vehicle, how to listen to music. For example, in a quintet, how to listen to and isolate completely an instrument, or which section is playing what. We'd close our eyes and follow every instrument individually, the base, strings, piano, brass and so on. Then we would bring them all together and it would 'blow your balls off'. That's why that bebop era of Donald Byrd, John Coltrane, Miles Davis and many others infiltrates me every time I hear it. Guy was teaching me how to dance without us dancing! I could dance to anything after that, rock, pop, jazz, soul, funk, hip-hop, classical it didn't matter as I was trained for hour upon hour of how to isolate and follow almost any beat, rhythm, tune or baseline.

## Zamba, business partner of the century

So each week when I went to The Sugar Reef I would promise myself one drink then home. Each week, as I was about to leave the DJ seemed to play one of those three or four favourite tunes that would convince me to stay. The next thing I knew, hours had passed and I was 'that guy', the last one on the dance floor, covered in sweat and topless. Damn, not that guy! One particular week I asked the DJ, who are you? He replied in a thick Italian accent, 'My name is Antonio.' I will never forget that look he gave me while he was talking, it was that kind of look which said 'I am manipulating you and there's nothing you can do about it,' and he was right! Perhaps this is the skill of every great DJ, to manipulate the audience in front of them with the tracks that they are laying down. But Antonio Zambarelli (or DJ Antonio Zalli, his DJ name back in the late eighties and early nineties) was different. Little did I know that four years from then, for sixteen years, the two of us would be the driving force behind some of the most noteworthy developments, which shaped Sydney's nightclub industry. As I had done with Bella during our almost twenty-year relationship, I learnt so much during this time, much of which came from him. Grazie Zamba!

# CHAPTER 17

# LONDON, IN DENIAL!

Returning to London was not in the plan and staying there for two years from 1994–96 even less so. I didn't want to leave Sydney and I was in denial all the way up to getting on the plane with one of my best friends to this day, Eric Chan, who accompanied me, including paying for my excess baggage…thanks Eric! I was broke, unhappy and I came home to grey, dark miserable London. I stayed with my Sister Carol (who I was at 3 The Ridgeway with) and even tried my hand at a corporate job in the city.

## Telesales misery, or was it?

This was probably one of the most soul-destroying jobs I have ever had! It comprised a few hundred people crammed into an office, calling up random people and trying to bypass the PA to get to the 'decision maker'. If you got through, then you had to sell them something and make a commission using a boring, repetitive and blatantly predictable script. I had a three-month trial period with a basic salary followed by commission only. I sat next to one guy who was the top salesman, Pany. This guy was a machine; he didn't cold call because he already had clients and referrals (he had been there for a year or so). He wouldn't stick to the script, he wrote his own. When he reached the key point of the conversation, when the sale was won or lost, he'd retreat under the table and proceed to shout at his prospect for five minutes then emerge from underneath the table with a smile and another successful sale. I learnt much from Pany even though I decided to leave after six months. What I learnt from him in a short period of time also proved invaluable to me years later.

## Modelling, dancing, acting – not singing!

I learnt a great deal from telesales, including that it wasn't really for me, and I was still broke so I supplemented my income for a short time, signing on the dole, or for supplementary benefits. During this time I was out looking for a model agent. I took my book that I had started in Australia to some of the well-known and not so well known agencies, eventually being accepted by Tracy at Manique Models. Fairly soon after that I was going on castings, attending parties, networking with other models and industry types.

During this time I carried a foolscap folder and inside I had plastic sleeves for holding business cards, at least sixteen per page. Within a year I had filled up two of the thickest foolscap folders worth of business cards. At every event, party, modelling job or function I would obtain up to five new business cards. On the back of each I wrote down where I met them, what we discussed and if I was supposed to get back to them at a certain time. Being this proactive, despite the fact I wasn't working much, created a high percentage of the jobs I did acquire. It was just like in Sydney a year or so prior, when with my friend, fellow model Walter Kennard, instead of waiting for castings we went and created our own opportunities. We knocked on doors, we approached casting agents when they were not even casting for jobs, we did our own tests, we found so many different ways to advance our opportunities, and it worked! In London, out of this time came commercials and a featured dancer role on *The Word* – a super hip Channel 4, magazine-type show that featured music acts and celebrity interviews, presented by Dani Behr and Terry Christian. I got that job through a great lady called Julie Dunne. I wasn't to know that years later Julie and I would work together on the MTV Music Awards in Milan, featuring Madonna. I became a widely used dancer/protagonist in film clips by acts such as, Womack & Womack, M People, Six Was Nine, Loveland '(Keep On) Shining', which we shot in Iceland, and I was cast with George Michael for 'Spinning The Wheel'.

**Franco – the photographer**

In London during this time I also attended a photography industry exhibition with a model friend called David. He was a mixed race, Caribbean, 6 feet tall but slight in stature, with a square jaw and the most amazing blue/brown eyes which sucked everyone in. Like Walter in Sydney, David and I were proactive, but still broke! I don't even remember the name of the exhibition but we heard there would be international photographers from Europe there who shot fashion, so as a long shot (we both wanted to get overseas) we went there with the intention of finding something that could help us in this regard. It was boring. Worse still, coming to the end of the exhibition we still had no real breakthroughs. Something drew me to a tall, rather gaunt, innocuous-looking fellow who smoked a lot. He had some portraits up which were neither here nor there but we struck up a conversation, by the end of which he said, 'If you ever come to Milano look me up', or words to that effect. I think both of us thought, well that wasn't going to happen, but common courtesy had probably kicked in as we were talking for half an hour and he felt somewhat duty-bound to make the offer. I placed his business card into one of the few remaining sleeves in my second foolscap folder, and that would probably be last I'd hear of him, I thought.

## Vijay – the designer

I don't really remember where I met Vijay (he'll probably kill me if he reads this). I would hazard a guess that it was a party or event where there were models. Vijay had an Indian background and was thin, square jawed, with very fine features and a small, off-white birthmark on his face. He was incredibly well spoken, intelligent and elegant, with a great sense of style. We struck up a conversation and I thought we got along well. Later, after becoming close friends, he would confide in me that he didn't like models, much less me at first! But somehow we kept seeing each other at events where we got to know each other better. Out of one these catch-ups he said he would be going to Milan and if I wanted to stay with him I'd be welcome. Take Franco above and now take Vijay and that word synchronicity* comes up again! It seems to have been following me through all of the years of my life when pursuing a seemingly insurmountable goal.

* According to the dictionary, synchronicity means the simultaneous occurrence of events that appear significantly related but have no discernible casual connection. Another way of seeing it is, whilst in pursuit of a dream or objective, those lucky coincidences, lucky breaks or sliding door moments which happen to you, the result of which can propel you massively towards achieving your goal or objective.

# CHAPTER 18

# OH MILANO!

In the summer of 1996, after two years in London where I think I had just had enough of just getting by or surviving, I decided if I was going to do this modelling thing I needed to go to Milan! So true to the can-do attitude for any escapade that I undertook, I proceeded to tell anyone that would listen of my intention, as if it had already happened. I consulted my foolscap folder of business cards for the two that mattered, Franco, the photographer and Vijay, the fashion designer. Then I checked my friend network and came up with a great friend and find, a tall, ginger-haired lad called David Townsend. I grew up with him through virtually all of my formative years at school and we played in the same sports teams too. I asked him if he knew anyone in Italy. He told me he had a great guy there called Riccardo, who worked in the coffee industry. Within a short period it was all organised and I could see it all unfolding in my mind: I'd go to Milan and stay with Vijay, see Franco to check up on modelling opportunities and catch up with Riccardo. Off on another adventure, I said goodbye to my sister and thanked her for letting me stay. A short flight later I found myself in Milan.

## Bring your funkiest wardrobe

Before I left London Vijay told me to bring my 'funkiest' wardrobe, so you can imagine how excited I was – Milan, modelling, fashion, funky wardrobe! 'I've got this' I told myself as I unpacked my suitcase at Vijay's apartment in Milan. It became rapidly apparent that I should have acquired 'his' definition of funky before packing. Immediately upon opening my case and setting an eye on what was inside Vijay quickly made two piles of clothes, an 'absolutely no way' and a 'possible' pile of clothes to wear in Milan. I think it was the pink shirt made for me for a very different purpose by then student designer and my girlfriend for a time, and a person I truly admire and respect, Genna Smart. It was a bright reddish pink with ruffles, exaggerated almost oversize sleeves and collar! If she's reading this (she's now a very successful designer on the world stage) she will laugh, as I am. Back to Vijay, I guess you could say I became more alarmed, teetering on the brink of embarrassment as nine-tenths of my specially selected funky wardrobe were in the first, to be destroyed, pile. I think I was left with one white, round neck T-shirt and a pair of pants! Vijay lent me one of his dark, V-neck jumpers to complete the ensemble and now I could set foot out in Milan!

## Go see Franco the photographer

I was meditating now, without a candle, not able to stop my thoughts but I was able to quieten my mind by focusing on my breath. I would sit comfortably, in a position which would not cause my knees to feel like they were about to pop! The only real rigour I committed to was to maintain a straight back. I would follow my breath in through my nose and all the way down into my lungs, pause, then slowly release it out of my mouth (or nose). I would practise as many mornings as I could and Vijay, a keen, lifelong meditator, also gave me advice and tips. I think I managed twenty minutes a sitting. Out of one of these meditations, after I'd been in Milan for a few days, came the direction to go see Franco, the photographer.

After navigating the confusing tram system in Milan (including getting lost numerous times) I chanced upon the address on the business card. As I pushed open that gate which opened out to a small piazza no more than five metres square, I couldn't help but think that I didn't remember what he looked like and self-doubt crept in: what was I thinking? I'm not a model! He probably won't even recognise me! Quite suddenly my thoughts were pierced by the sound of a door at the far end of the small courtyard opening to reveal a tall, well-dressed man carrying a suitcase. Was this Franco? I thought he was shorter. Time was running out as he was walking toward me and fairly soon he would be past me, out the gate and off to who knows where! I searched for empirical evidence, which was not forthcoming – I couldn't make out the number on the door he had come from and thus couldn't cross-check it with the number of where I was going. As he approached me he made no acknowledgment that he recognised me, let alone had spoken with me for half an hour. At least a year had passed since that trade show had taken place. Damn it! I had no choice, it was now or never, so in my best Italian accent I said 'Ciao, Franco?' Have you ever experienced that uncomfortable moment when someone doesn't speak to you, they just look you up and down, then up and down again like you are not supposed to be there? That's what I felt, a sense of horror! Finally he conceded, 'Si, sono Franco.'

## Breakthrough?

I had no response except to garble something in English about 'not speaking Italian' and worse still fumbled for the business card he gave me over a year ago in London from my foolscap folder! I wonder how this would have looked from the outside looking in. It was a warm Friday in Milan, I was wearing pants and a singlet. My body was in good shape due to all the boxing and kickboxing I had been doing. Little did I know, which he would later divulge, he was looking at the shape of my body when he was scanning me up and down. What I also didn't realise was that at that time male models had great bodies, as opposed to being waif like and androgynous. A man by the name of Marcus Schenkenberg was the embodiment of this look. More synchronicity!

## Testing, testing!

As it turned out, Franco was leaving his studio (which is where we were) to fly to New York on Monday, but importantly wasn't due back at his studio until after the trip. I still don't think he remembered me but we were now under a time pressure. I showed him my portfolio from Manique in London. He whipped through those pages in a flash, momentarily halting on a few body-shot type pictures. In his broken English I understood that we were going to do a shoot or a test – modelling shots for my book – right now! Then I was going to come back on Monday before he left for New York to look at the shots and basically go from there. He flung a series of wardrobe items at me to wear and intimated that I should be naked – no underwear. There is every chance the next sentence is going to come out wrong and you'll have an incorrect summation of me, so here goes. As a model, I was used to stripping off in front of people, but usually there is some thread of comfort with the person or group watching. Not here; but I could sense synchronicity at play and it was my break, so I didn't hesitate. Some of the pics are in this book.

## D–day Monday

As instructed, I returned on Monday to see Franco, who was in the final stages of developing the pictures from our shoot in his dark room. He asked for my book (portfolio), took pictures out, added pictures of our shoot in and sent me off to see a contact of his called Marco at Gay agency – I only caught the end of the name. The address he gave me wasn't far away and in a short period of time, I had got a much better handle on the Milanese trams (that is, I became lost less often than before!). I arrived at this Gay agency, a large, organised structure with a great deal of glass

(I think – these details are failing me now). I walked in without making eye contact with any of the male models I saw milling around talking; I was scared of the impending doom awaiting me. I was thinking of all different scenarios, each one worse than the next. What would I be prepared to do to make it in Milan? How far would I be prepared to go? The 'Get naked' shoot with Franco was just the beginning, I thought! I was not confident, and even that was an understatement, fearful is more accurate. I found my way to Marco in the quickest possible time.

## Sign here

I sat down in front of Marco, a handsome mixed-race man, and told him Franco had sent me. Marco was the men's booker – the person who finds you work. I sat down in front of him, still nervous but acting cool and confident. I handed over my book which he tore through at a rate of knots, just like Franco did. I thought I'd be shown the door soon enough. To my surprise a few pieces of paper were placed in front of me that I was asked to fill out and sign.

Seemingly at the speed of light, in my mind I summed my situation up: I was broke, in a foreign country where I had only spent a short period of time and didn't speak the language, I was staying in a share apartment with a guy who didn't really like me, I just got my kit off for a weirdish kind of man and now I was in an agency called Gay something or other and an induction form was being put under my nose for me to fill in the detail and join the agency! Unashamed, I did what any other model looking

151

to make it would do – I signed everything straight away without delay! Marco, gave me details of where to get the composites (model business cards) completed and to call him every day for castings first thing in the morning. I got up and probably shook his hand (I don't remember – still in shock about what I'd just potentially said yes to) and left.

### Riccardo Gay – Model Plan

It was on the way out that my eye wandered up one of the walls filled with magazine covers – *Vogue, Elle, Marie Claire* and so on – of the models' work who were with the agency. I almost fell over when I saw Naomi Campbell, Linda Evangelista, Eva Herzigová, Christy Turlington, Marcus Schenkenberg and more. They were the supermodels of that era who were being represented by the same agency that I was now part of! It wasn't 'Gay' it was pronounced 'Guy' as in Riccardo Gay – it seems that a mix of, not really paying attention and the Italian pronunciation got the better of me. I was now being represented by one of the best agencies in Milan, in arguably one of the most crucial fashion hubs in the world...I couldn't believe it!

In other words, if I hadn't attended that trade show/ exhibition and met Franco, had I not met Vijay (who offered to put me up for a short time) so decided not to go to Milan, if I hadn't left that day to see Franco, or spoken up whilst walking across that little piazza, and been willing to get even more uncomfortable by doing a shoot or test there...well then, it is very unlikely this would have happened! Try to calculate the odds of that synchronicity!

## Model success

In one year with Ricardo Gay – Model Plan, I worked with the supermodels on various fashion shows. Amongst many others I worked for Romeo Gigli, Bata, Versace, Allen Cox Underwear and in television on *I Guastefeste* as the lead protagonist. I was on the front cover of *Pellicce Moda,* in a billboard campaign throughout Italy for Mueller yoghurt and many more.

## Italians

By the end of the first of my two years in Italy I was learning Italian culture and the insatiable Italian ability to package a product and ultimately sell it. Anglo Saxon culture, from how I grew up in England, was reserved, and a lot of the time, being extroverted, I found myself playing the role of a circle trying to fit into a square. In Italy, being extroverted – hand gesturing, facial expressions fuelled with passion – seemed to be the modus operandi of the majority of the population, and this alone made the extroverted side of my personality feel instantly at home. To this extent I had half the language, the body language, covered. Learning the other half, the verbal, was all I had to do and I was so supremely motivated I was speaking fluently within a year.

The second thing I was taken aback by in Italy was their ability to sell by making whichever product, quite frankly, sexy! One clear example was the way in which both sexes, men and women, dressed and held themselves. They made the most of what they had by accentuating the positives and minimising or disguising the negatives and the end result was beauty in motion. Cars, furniture, houses and art, the list could be endless – they just knew inherently how to sell and it was infectious.

### Good Lord *Immagine* (pronounced Ima-gin-neh)

*immagine*

<u>feminine noun</u>

a. (*gen*) (also physics) image

b. (*rappresentazione, fotografia*) picture

> **una bella immagine** a nice picture
>
> **è l'immagine della salute** he's the picture of health

I met models from other agencies on castings and at functions and one in particular, Marco, was as keen to improve his English as I was to learn Italian, and we hit it off right away. Marco informed me about companies who supplied models to do special guest appearances in nightclubs. Essentially the nightclub was 'renting a crowd' by paying models to be there, which in turn would attract a crowd to their venue, with the notion they could meet international models there. Remember, we are talking about the mid-to-late nineties now, and yes, these days with social media, endorsement by superstars with gazillions of followers in some ways mimics this, but in Italy it was happening decades before I was there. Ten or more of us would meet in a central location in Milan late afternoon on the weekends, divide ourselves into cars and drive anywhere from two to five hours to reach our destination where we would be treated to dinner with drinks by the venue, work, and return the next morning with a large amount of cash in our pockets. By work, essentially it was being paid for a night out! We would drink, interact with locals, dance, enjoy ourselves and not pay a cent from our pocket. I had to pinch myself on more than several occasions. My life for a time comprised modelling during the week and *immagine* on the weekends, which would give me cashflow while waiting for modelling-job money to come in.

## *Animatore* opportunity (pronounced ani–ma–tor–eh)

*animatore*

<u>noun</u>

noun: **entertainer**; plural noun: **entertainers**

1. a person, such as a singer, dancer, or comedian, whose job is to entertain others.

Though my Italian was good, it still wasn't quite up to scratch at that point, so I would spend more time on the dancefloor than standing around talking to people. Often a circle would form and I would unleash a crazy series of moves that would draw favourable attention – it was like a show! After one of these nights, on the drive back in the car Marco told me about 'podium dancing'. I was laughing, as in my head I'd conjured up images of a scantily clad go-go dancers on a podium in a strip club! But no, according to Marco, podium dancing, was not only a profession in Italy at that time, but highly paid too. Professional dancers were doing it. Three sets of around twenty minutes each including three changes of costume around the peak times of the night could earn me five times the amount which I earned doing *immagine*. If you were really talented, even more than that!

### Another lucky break

It didn't take long for me to think this one over. My modelling work, even though I secured some high-profile and some high-paying jobs, was so inconsistent. My regular cashflow was coming from *immagine*. Within weeks, the same agency which booked me for the *immagine* jobs was now booking me for the *animatore* jobs and indeed I did earn more than three, sometimes five times as much. But then I got an even luckier break.

One of the commercials I was part of in England was sold for European distribution and when it came to Italy it was extremely well received. As I mentioned, Italians know how to package and sell better than anyone else (in my opinion). I was now sold as a celebrity *animatore*: Robert Ian Bonnick from Grundig.

Over my final year in Italy I became one of the highest paid and most recognised *animatore* throughout Italy on the back of that Grundig commercial, which opened more doors to me than I can even remember. I worked in the biggest, best and most famous clubs throughout Italy from as far north as Bergamo and Bolzano, as far east as Venice and Riccone and as far south as Calabria. For two summers I was invited, by the Gennaro/Pfister family who owned one of the most famous venues in Italy, Byblos Disco Dinner Club just outside of Riccione. What was the role? To occupy the very highly coveted position of resident, with La Veronique, a sexy black girl from France.

## Byblos Disco Dinner Club

Located in the hills of Misano Monte, Byblos looks down onto the seaside town of Riccione, a few kilometres away. Born in 1971, it is a magnificently constructed large, luxury Mediterranean-style villa with ornate patios, balconies, porches and rooves typical of that style. It is self-contained, housing its own gourmet restaurant, which later becomes a nightclub with its own parking and field opposite, where helicopters dropping off and picking up international dignitaries and celebrities come and go.

Riccione takes in the coastline of the Adriatic Sea and is very close to Rimini. In the nineties Rimini/Riccione formed one of the party capitals, like Ibiza is now. Veronique and I created dance shows, catwalks, entertained and maintained the public relations with some of the most famous celebrities, sports stars, actors, politicians, models and dancers in Italy and beyond – it was like our playground. Looking back, I would be hard pushed to find many experiences which matched those summers at Byblos. I was provided a red Vespa, apartment nearby, meals up at the house and was paid on top of that!

In such a short space of time I had managed to rise to the top while having the time of my life. One thing I noticed on the journey was that most dancers/entertainers didn't really make contact with the patrons, they would stay in their own world for the twenty to thirty minute set, get down and go to the green room. What I did was engage the patrons, laugh, chat and joke, jump off the podium to dance with them and sometimes I would pull them up to dance with me – I wouldn't really discriminate either, sometimes it was alpha males, sometimes girls. In between the sets I wouldn't go off to the green room, I would stay and talk to people, have shots and so on. This led to time spent after or outside working hours with some of the patrons, a number of whom were high profile, others no profile. I believe that this attitude is what led me to build a network very deep and very fast throughout Italy, which led to so many experiences I look back on and smile, like the ones below.

## I Guastafeste – Il Nigeriano!

Italy is a country, much like England, which is football (or calcio) crazy! Actually, the word obsessed comes a little close to the truth. Italy as a football nation has always punched well above its weight, producing one of the most successful footballing nations in the world. The Italian team has won the FIFA World Cup four times, trailing only Brazil (with five), as well as being runners-up in two finals and reaching a third place.

Italy's top domestic football league, the Serie A, is one of the most popular professional sports leagues in the world. Italy's club sides have won 48 major European trophies, making them the second most successful nation in European football. Serie A hosts three of the world's most famous clubs in Juventus, Milan and Inter.

So imagine my joy (and trepidation) when in 1996 I was offered a the feature role on an episode of one the most famous shows on Italian television called *I Guastafeste,* hosted by Massimo Lopez and Luca Barbareschi. Massimo is an actor and director, known for *I Promessi Sposi* (1990) and *Zootopia* (2016) among others. Luca is also an actor and producer, known for *The International* (2009), and *The Mercury Conspiracy* (2013).

A great way to picture *I Guastafeste* would be as the *Candid Camera* (hidden camera/practical joke reality television series) of Italy. The part I played was of a highly touted, arrogant and overly confident imported football player from Nigeria. I was given the name Robert Raku Ponnick by the producers. This was at a time when Nigerian football players playing in Serie A like George Weah were very well received and highly prized as players, especially the strikers or centre forwards. The team targeted for this ruse was Castel di Sangro in Serie B.

Castel di Sangro were a team with ambitions to go up to Serie A. Their hopes were given a tremendous boost with the signing of a gun centre forward from the English Premier League team of Leicester City. Three groups of people were in on it and the rest, including the manager of Castel di Sangro, the board, supporters, media and people of the town, nestled into the hills of Abruzzo, had no idea. At the time there were many articles, some very controversial. I have included translated excerpts from a later article (dated 4 January 2015) from the Italian website CalcioNews24.com entitled 'The Ponnick Hoax'.

***The biggest charade of Italian football: the purchase (or presumed) of Robert Raku Ponnick by Castel di Sangro***

When Castel di Sangro in November 1996 bought the Nigerian Robert Raku Ponnick few would have thought of a joke.

…Castel di Sangro announces the coup to the press. Robert Raku Ponnick arrives, a powerful Nigerian striker who plays in the Premier League in Leicester City. It's 1996, few can afford the internet and Wikipedia has not yet been invented, so we trust the hearsay: Ponnick is a great tip.

It took place over two days and the scale of it was truly something to behold. I had media follow me in from the airport and to and from press conferences. It made the news in all the mainstream media such as *La Reppublica,* I conducted television interviews all while in the character of the bigheaded, somewhat rude and disrespectful Robert Raku Ponnick. The interviews were shown throughout Italy on the most watched football shows and sports reports. They bought it.

…Ponnick opts for a resounding monologue: 'It's better that the inhabitants of Castel-whatever be careful, if you care about your women leave them in the house, if they are cute I do them all and I do not care who I am.

The next day I played in a friendly which was watched by the local supporters. Only the team in the dressing room

# Jackson plays it cool on the dance floor

By Sydney Confidential's
PETER HOLDER

STAND aside, Anthony Mundine — the (real) Man is in town.

Samuel L Jackson, in Sydney to shoot scenes for George Lucas's Stars Wars: Episode II, cut a cool, fine figure on Saturday night, letting off steam at a crowded dance party.

Without the usual star trappings of an entourage laden with burly bodyguards, Jackson happily mingled and danced with the hip Sydney set at House Solution, a dance party held at the Wharf 8 shipping terminal.

With two rooms of music, Jackson gravitated to the one playing the sexier, funkier tunes. By his side for most of the night was classically trained Sydney dancer Nikki Fantl, 24. Both stayed on the dance floor for a couple of frenzied hours.

One partygoer, Kristen Serra, said she was stunned to find herself dancing next to one of the world's most popular and hardest-working actors.

"He was really cool and was just getting down and having a good time just like everyone else," she said.

"He fitted right in."

Jackson — who also stars in Shaft, which opens nationally in a fortnight — arrived in Sydney last Wednesday to prepare for the action scenes in Episode II. Within hours of arriving, he played 18 holes of golf at Moore Park.

Resting up . . . Samuel L. Jackson with his dancing partner Nikki Fantl at the weekend, and (inset) on the dance floor.   Picture: JAMIE FAWCETT

Legendary actor Samuel L Jackson (with Nicole Fantl) came to one of our Sydney House Solution events in 2000.

Grammy award winning DJ/producers Masters At Work – Kenny Dope and Louie Vega – played at our NYE 2012 event in Sydney.

With TV celebrity Laura Csortan at a media launch in Sydney. With TV celebrity Laura Csortan at a media launch in Sydney.

With actor Justin Melvey at a Sydney media launch.

Pictured here with one of most successful swimmers of all time Ian Thorpe, and one of the most successful producer/DJs of all time Frankie Knuckles aka The 'Godfather Of House Music', who played at one of our events at Zeta Sydney (Hilton Sydney).

## VANITY
THE AGENCY

Level 1, 729 Elizabeth Street, Waterloo NSW 2017. Phone: (02) 319 3145  Fax: (02) 699 3183

ROBERT BONNICK

| Height 6'3 | Chest 42" | Waist 33" | Suit 42L |
| Hair Black | Eyes Brown | Shoe 12 | |

My very first modelling composite card in Sydney during the early nineties when I had hair!

A heady mix of entertainment forms under one roof is being touted as a cultural alternative to the nightclub. **CAITLIN WRIGHT** reports

Two major nightclub names are venturing into uncharted territory with their next project, *House Solution*.

Antonio Zambarelli and Robert Ian Bonnick, the creators of Home nightclub, promise to combine key aspects of Sydney culture with the party atmosphere of European resort Ibiza and the variety of the Hong Kong markets.

*House Solution* appears to be an entirely different night-life alternative. It is aimed at 20 to 35-year-olds wanting a stimulating event to frequent. The plan is to place a variety of entertainment forms in spaces of their own, under one roof.

The obvious attraction will be the 2000sq m music area. In the next six months, Zambarelli plans to host the best DJs from France, Italy, the UK and America. The first event will feature Italian producers Blade and Alex Neri.

The music, however, is only the beginning. The rest of the complex will cater for other cultural senses.

In one corner, there will be a film room, which screens current and past releases. Another sectioned-off corner will feature a photographic exhibition of the contemporary urban environment. Also in the vicinity will be some of Versace's most important works in *The Versace Exhibition*.

Elsewhere, renowned chefs Neil Perry (The Rockpool Group) and Simon Goh (Chinta Ria) will provide food for a relaxed lounge area.

Zambarelli and Bonnick say *House Solution* is the first event of its kind in the world. They want to encapsulate Greenwich Village's "sense of freedom" and they believe Sydney is just the place to launch it.

"In Sydney, we are doing better than anywhere else," Zambarelli said. "We have nine months of perfect weather and the people are very funky."

It is the so-called "funky people" who will make or break *House Solution*. According to Bonnick and Zambarelli, there's already high interest.

Their previous events organisation experience, as

# HOMEboys

directors of EnE AcA Special Events, built their reputations. Before the creation of Home, Zambarelli saw the need for a different type of club for the Sydney scene.

Italian-born Zambarelli was the DJ and entrepreneur with a self-confessed "good eye for detail". Despite living in Sydney for the past 13 years, he has spent much of this time jet-setting between performances in Australia, Italy and Spain.

He met Bonnick, an English-born Jamaican, 10 years ago while DJ-ing in a Sydney club. Despite Bonnick returning to the UK a short time later, they remained in contact, and worked together on Home.

*House Solution* will cater for a different clientele from Home, they say. Subtitled *Intelligent Evenings For A Discerning Crowd*, it's aiming to be more of a cultural experience than the average nightclub. And you might get something rarely seen at nightclubs.

"It goes back to customer service," Zambarelli says. "If we can do that and do that properly, then the customers will come back."

*House Solution*, a monthly event, plays the Wharf 8 Shipping Terminal, Walsh Bay on July 8.

picture: **CHRIS HYDE**

Daily Telegraph 1998 feature section on Home nightclub with Zamba and me.

**FIVE WAY FUSION**

205 Glenmore Rd Paddington
NSW 2021 Australia
Ph 331 2828
Fax 360 2504

Photograph for FWF
by Helmut Gensen

Gianni Versace lycra boxer shorts and
black bath towel with gold embroidered
medusa head.

Model: R.I.B. courtesy Ursula Hufnagl
Chic Model Management

LOUD Advertising 958 6564

One of my most memorable first modelling jobs in Sydney in the early 1990s for Paul Jellard of Five Way Fusion wearing Gianni Versace. Shot by Helmut Jensen and styled by Benedicta.

The team that made clubbing history in Sydney at Tank nightclub. From left to right, me, Zamba and Paul Nicolarakis, shot at Zeta Bar during one of our club nights.

My first greetings card (global release) care of the Ink Group in London during the 1990s. Yes, I had dreads! Well, little ones!

Both taken by Peter Gravelle for the Swish Jeans parade in Milan during Italian Fashion Week (late 1990s), my first show with one of the supermodels.

The biggest, love, focus, passion and source of drive and personal growth in my life, my family, from left to right my partner (Super Mum/Business Woman), Marina Agustina, our eldest daughter Alexa-Rose Bonnick, myself and our youngest daughter Almira-Sava Bonnick.

knew that I had also incensed one of the two current strikers – who at that time weren't scoring any goals – in another disrespectful act to make them feel that I was coming in to take their spot in the team:

> …Castel di Sangro is not very well placed and has strong problems in attack, the poor Gauls and Pistella do not score…

The joke was finally revealed in the stadium with the crowd looking on. I still have a copy of the footage, the look on some of those faces in the crowd is of pure disbelief – I still remember the reaction of adults and kids alike. They felt cheated and deeper down inside me, after the euphoria of the success, and pressure of holding to a character that grated me deeply was over, I too began to lament – but tried to push those feelings aside at the time. These were real people who thought something big was going to happen, something which they came out to see and support.

I haven't really thought more about it until writing this book and whilst searching online for some footage and articles it hit me…Ponnick is no longer heard of, nor a picture nor a video remain in the vast world of the internet today. Maybe it's better this way.

When the joke became less newsworthy and was swept under the carpet in the proverbial sense after the show aired on Silvio Berlusconi's Canale 5 network, I was reading that it had some real negative impacts. Not only were people taken for a ride, there were shake-ups with management, a player was sold to make way for Ponnick and other less fortunate events also later occurred which I won't go into here. At the time of writing this there are a few articles still up on the internet if you're interested to read on.

As a once budding actor playing a role, the synchronicity of being in Italy where football is regarded so highly, at the right time, reminds me of how fortunate and lucky I have been considering that my goal (and the objective of every actor/*animatore*) was for exposure on the highest stage. However from a human perspective, and that of my conscience, I don't know if I would have taken that opportunity in hindsight.

## Bobby

Though what follows happened a year later, it seems ironic that we are staying with football, in Italy. Bobby (not his real name), in the late 1990s used to come to Byblos with some of the other football players in the Italian national team. I liked Bobby – we always got along well, and on occasion he would invite me to go out with all or some of this crew, which comprised some of the most well-known and famous football players in Italy and Europe at the time, including captain of Italian football team, Paolo Maldini, and many others. We'd go to a few other clubs that thumped around that time such as La Pineta in Milano Marittima and Villa Della Rose also in Riccione, attend special events and private parties.

Later Bobby would be named by one of the greatest footballers of our time, Pele, in the FIFA 100, a list of the 125 greatest living footballers, as part of FIFA's centenary celebrations. Though the official move wasn't until 1999, I was with Bobby the night he got confirmation of his transfer to Lazio for a record breaking £32 million (€43 million), which made him the richest football player in the world!

When I look back on the final piece to this story, I shake my head and laugh! I was given a red Vespa each summer I worked at Byblos. That particular night I was inebriated but coherent, if that makes any sense, and I was about to ride the 3 to 4 kilometres down the hill (including switchbacks) into Riccione. As usual, I was to meet all of the football gang there, as they usually had drivers. Bobby, who was also in a merry state, shouted, 'Rob I'm coming with you!'

So try to picture this, a shy yet extroverted, lanky, drunk kid who grew up penniless in two children's homes in London zigzagging the 3 or 4 kilometres down a steep hill with switchbacks into Riccione in the early hours of the morning with 'the richest football player in the world' on the back! But then he hadn't signed yet. What if we had crashed?! Someone up there must be looking after me!

## Madonna miss, for Sydney opportunity

Back in London I mentioned that I worked as a dancer on a show called *The Word*. Julie Dunne was the lady who employed me and the other 'talent'. Julie had Thick black hair, pale skin, fine features and a nose ring. If she would follow a political party it would probably be the Greens. Not too tall, or small for that matter, she had the kind of disposition which said 'If you do right by me not only will I back you but I'll go in to battle for you. If you try to be smart, conniving or try to screw me I will cut you off in a heartbeat!' And she did precisely that; I saw it many times! When she heard I was going to Italy to pursue modelling she was the kind of person who said keep in touch…and she did.

One such occasion was when she was in charge of talent/casting for the MTV Music Awards in Milan, featuring Madonna in 1998. Whenever you see a show on TV where there are studio guests, audience or featured talent such as dancers, models, actors or extras you will find a talent or casting director working tirelessly behind the scenes. Often the unsung heroes or heroines, they can work late into the night or even into the morning. But without them most of the shows on TV would have no following, it's like trying to make a movie without using actors. Pointless! Not only that but they have to work to unforgiving deadlines too! She got in touch and asked me to be the Italian connection, as she knew I was a networker, with my two white foolscap folders! I connected her up to Italian celebrities, models, dancers, actors and nightclub impresarios who formed part of the featured and non-featured talent which appeared on the MTV Music Awards.

I was due to be there in person to oversee and be part of the talent that could be featured alongside the special guest, Madonna. An opportunity to meet one of my heroines went begging due to one call from Sydney from

Antonio, and a bigger opportunity that awaited me there. Unfortunately, the timing for me couldn't have been worse – I would have to be in two places at once! So I had to choose and I chose Sydney. More about that shortly.

### Write your memoir

I'm beginning to understand how cathartic it is to look back and write your memoir, not necessarily to include in a book, though why not, but because you really will get a sense as to how lucky you have been. I'm not necessarily referring to the incredible experiences you have had with loved ones, complete strangers, celebrities, or your next door neighbour. We all go through times of being up and being down. By going through this exercise you will find so many things that you have done to be proud of and an awareness of your patterns – do you hide away when confronted with problems? Do you only think of the positive, or do you face problems head on? There is no right or wrong here – it will just give you clarity. Once you know what you are dealing with, then you can do something about it! As a father of two young girls, I can say that if you have kids, it will give you insights into how you were brought up or what you went through. Most importantly you'll probably see those same patterns repeating now with your kids. Except, you have an opportunity now to be more conscious in how you are bringing them up. But failing all else, it will give your self-esteem a positive nudge to get through some tough times, if that's what you're going through now. Looking back at your past can keep you on track if all is working successfully, or kick you off the fence you're sitting on or if you're stuck. I really encourage you to do it!

## Lessons to learn

With all the people I have met over the years, rich and famous, poor and destitute, privileged or underprivileged, white or black, old or young and so on, the one constant I have always seen is that we all have our own specific challenges we come into life with.

Our choice is, firstly, whether we choose to acknowledge them and secondly, if we choose to do what is necessary to overcome them. How something or someone appears on the outside doesn't mean you know what is happening with them on the inside. One of Sydney's famous restaurateurs, a young, upwardly mobile, generous, handsome really lovely man who had (from the outside looking in) a successful business in a very tough industry took his own life. At the time of writing this three celebrity chefs have been in the news recently who took the same path. We seem to be immersed or stuck in Insta-consciousness. Please don't misunderstand me, I use social media, mobile devices and watch TV (less now). But when people actually start to believe the so-called life that a large majority of the social media users – according to what they post – are apparently having, it sets up an expectation that I feel cannot be satisfied. This in turn leads to being down on yourself and at worst, depressed.

In my life already I have made so many mistakes as a result of this 'looking good' affliction – credit card debts, repossessed vehicle, relationship breakdowns. Fortunately, I have enough other experiences, such as meditation with masters, self-development courses, good friends courageous enough to tell me the truth and supportive partners. All this forces me to realise my outside world is a reflection of my inside world. When I take this on board I stop blaming other people and looking for the solutions to my challenges 'out there' but in here, or within me. Through practice, failing but getting up again, my mastery of this is improving.

# CHAPTER 19

# SYDNEY, THE RETURN LEG

If it wasn't for the last-minute organising of the ticket by Antonio I might not have made it back to Sydney. I was sweating it! 'I leave Madonna behind for this?' I thought! Home nightclub in Sydney was a more than $10 million development which included the Royal Bank of Scotland and three other major partners. It was the first superclub in the Southern Hemisphere (the first purpose-built 3000-plus capacity venue). My role of special event manager/VIP manager and a 457 four-year working visa awaited me.

I was on a roll and I knew it. My luck was holding, even when there was a last-minute mix-up and I had no ticket to fly till the very last moment, like a groom waiting at the altar, slowly beginning to wonder if he was about to be stood up by his bride, when suddenly she appears!

At first, I had a sense of expectancy, of great things to come. It felt good, even though I didn't know fully what I was doing! On the other hand, I was also filled with self-doubt and dread; a fear that I might be discovered, or found out to be a fraud! But slowly I found my way, with Antonio at the helm and backing me up.

I realised quickly that Antonio had the vision and I was the front person. I remember first walking into Tank nightclub in Sydney on a site visit and he asked me what I thought of it as a venue and I said I didn't like it. He told me that it would probably be the best thing we would ever do, and he was right! I remember our launch on the Australia Day weekend like it was yesterday. I was standing at the top of the steps down to the main dance floor, looking onto what seemed like a sea of people moving in unison like a Mexican wave around a football stadium, the music thumping, the crowd pulsating. We were way over capacity, with hundreds still waiting outside. I was scared! I had the same feeling when I went to my first Arsenal football game, a fierce local derby. I was in the stands with thousands of other people. I stand over six feet tall with an athletic build, but we were packed so tightly that I couldn't move. I was totally at the mercy of what the crowd wanted to do as I couldn't fight free. If the crowd moved left I would move left! If the crowd moved right then so would I. I was petrified! Only with deep breathing and focus was I able to bring my breath, my body and my senses back under control. Walking down those steps to get to the DJ booth to announce our special guest I felt the same fear.

We worked as a solid team and with each venue we became sharper, stronger, smarter; like trapeze artists letting go in mid-air, knowing that the other would be there to catch me and vice versa.

The launch of Home Sydney in 1998, was followed

by Housesolution – 'the warehouse party for grown-ups', according to Jackie Dent in *The Sydney Morning Herald*. Then there was Tank nightclub between 2001 and 2005, which was voted one of the top-three clubs in the world, and finally Zeta Bar Sydney from 2005 to 2012. We created history in Sydney primarily because we had the know-how, the trust, the motivation, the execution and the belief!

Those twenty years gave me so much more than I bargained for; times of great joy, sadness and gratitude. I got to hang out, party and talk with some of my greatest idols one-on-one such as Samuel L Jackson, Laurence Fishburne, Ian Thorpe and Jennifer Hawkins to name a few. Take Ian for instance…

## Thorpey

During that time of becoming the most successful swimmer of the modern era, I met Ian Thorpe through mutual friends. During those years I also met and chaperoned many celebrities and high-profile visitors to and within the various nightspots we were running throughout that time in Sydney such as Home, Tank and Zeta Bar. Some of these stars also became friends during that time.

Ian and I would soon discover we were born on the same day, 13 October, and over a three-year or so period would join each other's groups to celebrate. Standing a little taller, with a thicker build than me, we had some things in common. He had a massive heart, was very generous, intuitive, possessing a high degree of emotional intelligence, and could get along with and inspire just about anyone.

I was always impressed by how he is a lifetime learner, a student of whatever he is focused on, such as swimming for example. I can swim, though I wouldn't call myself a strong swimmer, but I learnt through a few conversations how seriously he studied through seeking out and selecting specialists in related and seemingly unrelated fields who could help him get more out of his body and swim more efficiently. Things like the angle at which his hands sliced through the water, creating as much surface area as possible once in the water to propel him through it with great speed. He had so much elegance when in the water, when training, when in competition or when I saw him on TV. Blessed with hindsight I would liken his way of swimming to the way Roger Federer goes about his business of playing tennis on and off the court! I remember one piece of advice he gave to me in relation to doing more of the things for a living which engaged my heart. He knew, as I did at that time, I really needed to get back on to my purpose of uplifting and inspiring people.

Probably the most valuable gift that I learnt through spending some quality time with people in general, whether they have a profile or not, is that we all have our own specific challenges in our life and it's up to us to recognise and respect them BEFORE overcoming them. One of my major challenges in life is the feeling of belonging, or lack thereof. I have always felt like an imposter of sorts, who doesn't really fit in anywhere. I can become close to people very quickly but I can also have a tendency to push people away if they get too close.

## Who is my tribe?

I first played the role of the comedian growing up in children's homes to avoid being beaten, bullied or hurt. Then came the chameleon, blending in to almost any environment in order to be liked. Now having two kids and a loving partner is finally giving me a sense of belonging; I know who my tribe is. Do you know what your specific challenges in life are? Have you ever thought about them?

As a young man I still had questions. I was shy and felt out of my depth, I identified with being white not black, not confident, at times very, very down, usually about how I looked. Over the next twenty-five years my life changed dramatically but 3 The Ridgeway, and all of my experiences there, created the person I was to become and gave me the fuel to drive the change I so badly wanted. I'm so incredibly grateful to all of the people there, both members of staff and children alike. I learnt from all of you. Many years since I left 3 The Ridgeway, I still live by this mantra:
1. Never forget where I'm from;
2. Never forget those who have helped me become who I am today;
3. I continue to pass on what I have learnt to others and through this I developed the five keys, which when mastered allow you to achieve your 'true' heart goals!

# PART 5
# THE FIVE KEYS

## Introduction

You now know a sufficient amount about where I came from. The second part of this book goes into what, how, why and who influenced me to really step up. The following and final piece of the puzzle is separated into five sections, each one representing one of the five keys. I found I could consistently manifest my 'true' heart goals whenever I followed them. If I didn't achieve them, it was due to not truly following the steps, or it wasn't truly my heart's desire to do so.

## Heart goal

When I set the intention to find a life partner I remember setting up an image, a picture of what I wanted, in great detail. I got into the height, weight, look, hair colour, the list goes on. But what I found wasn't the superficial, it was actually what my heart desired – someone I could have a family with, rely upon, love, trust and who would be a strong role model for family.

## Tripping up on the road to success

Making it this far you have done yourself and myself a great honour, as you are either truly committed to change, having a laugh with (or at) me, interested in what happened in my life or all of the above! Either way, as promised, I'm going to put it all together for you and give you the opportunity to road test the five keys for yourself at the same time. As we go through you'll see that I used them time and time again to deliver a consistent result, every time.

I am a lifetime learner and in the time since writing

the book I've continued to update what I'm doing, reading and road testing. This book explains which processes or modalities that I was using at that time – which still work today if you follow them! This is because the five key areas identified remain the same. The key drivers are also the same, such as how much you want to or are willing to change to reach your objective, the compelling reasons why you want to achieve it (which creates the fearless outlook of feeling unstoppable), being able to use all your senses to visualise yourself with clarity already achieving your dream, recognising the role of taking action, accepting the role synchronicity plays, the ability to stay on track and deal with challenges, and finally, accepting the role that time plays.

Keeping this in mind, now let's move on!

Let me remind you (and me) of how far we have come. Step by step you have seen me emerge from a cocoon of sorts, like a larva becoming a butterfly. You have seen my flaws, my mistakes, some of my successes; you've seen an insatiable desire to keep learning, to keep moving forward and above all not to give up. I've conveyed these to you for two reasons: number one, you have these traits too – we all do! And number two, which is the essential message of this book, no matter where you're from or what your background you can have success, overcome adversity, achieve and become a better you in the process! It's just about having a roadmap to guide you there and this is what this part of the book is all about. For the best results, take time to consider and fill in the answers to the questions as honestly and authentically as you can. The more honest you are the deeper the transformation.

To make this section more valuable I will demonstrate two examples of this process and actually work through each of them using the five keys. Let's say for example you divide your life dreams into five different areas: relationship dreams, financial dreams, career dreams, sport dreams and health dreams. I suggest you work on one area at a time for a minimum of three months, starting with the most pressing first. I will choose two and work on each to show you how I did it. The two examples I will work on will be my sport and relationship dreams.

My sport dream was to play basketball for the England under-15 basketball team.

My relationship dream was to find a strong partner, who I was attracted to, could inspire and support me to achieving my goals and who I could raise a family with.

So let me take you through the five-step process with the two dreams above.

Your life has purpose.
Your story is important.
Your dreams count.
Your voice matters.
You were born to make
an impact!

# GET YOURSELF A DREAM OR BETTER STILL A PURPOSE!

### Key 1 and my sport dream

When I was asked at the age of fourteen, what I wanted to do with my life in terms of career, at that time I would envy those people around me who could answer that question succinctly, as I didn't know. However, when it came to sport I already had my answer, to play basketball for the England under-15 basketball team.

I was introverted at home (3 The Ridgeway) most of the time and didn't really engage. This set me back in that my confidence and self-esteem were not developing, but it also gave me one very important advantage. I could see the choices my fellow orphans were making and where those choices led them. The longer I stayed at 3 The Ridgeway and saw people fail the more I wanted to succeed. Lee… dead, Jackie…dead, my fellow orphans, some of whom had taught me so much, were failing BIG time! For the first time I started to think I needed to succeed for them. Without any pressure from them or the members of staff,

I started to feel a sense of responsibility. I wanted to show them that the time they spent to teach me football, tennis, dancing or how to stick up for myself, to name but a few, wasn't wasted. In the early years I really didn't know if anyone thought I would amount to anything anyway. Nonetheless, this was probably the first time I actually began to realise that the truly powerful people focus on what's best for others as opposed to just themselves.

## Sport – gateway to courage

In the pursuit of sport, in this case playing basketball for England under-15s, was one of the first times I tripped across the entire process of creating success without even realising it. Remember when I told you in the earlier chapters why I loved sport? It didn't matter where you were from, your background, colour, level of education, birthright – it was a level playing field. I saw it as my way to be who I wanted to be; I was free to express myself the way I wanted to without being worried or concerned about what other people thought.

I didn't really hear so much the voice inside my head, inside all of our heads, the self-talk that is running your life and won't shut up; do this, do that, this person is full of crap or full of that. What's your little voice in your head telling you right now?

## Key 1 and my relationship dream

When it came to relationships the answer came many years later but 3 The Ridgeway once again gave me my purpose. In the first place there was my own situation of being placed in the children's home for which I don't blame my parents. I have realised the difficulty of bringing up kids, the strain it can cause to a relationship, even without postnatal depression. The financial burden! The physical burden! The lack of sleep! Add to this the fact that my parents were far from home, in a country foreign to them, with no income, support or prospects to fall back on. I have now witnessed all of this personally as a parent and a person who has lived in foreign countries where I didn't initially speak the language.

Whilst at 3 The Ridgeway I experienced and saw for myself firsthand the effects of inappropriate parenting, or complete lack of parenting. I saw how the kids turned out and I saw how my sister and I turned out. We grew up in the same environment but have very different results when it comes to intimate relationships. In the same way as I was driven to succeed in achieving my sporting dreams, having a family and a relationship that works, without divorce or breaking up, consumed me. I didn't want my kids growing up in a children's home or separated from their parents.

I found my supportive, inner self-talking companion at the age of twelve. You may recall I told you how I literally thought I was white for my first fourteen years of life due to being the only black kid at school for the entire time. I would go to my room, bring out the mirror and put it up to my face. I hated my nose – too wide for my thin face! I thought my lips were too big and my pointy head too unsymmetrical. In short, I felt ugly. Hours would go by and I'd still be there lying on my bed crying. I felt like looks were the most important thing and didn't have them! I was ugly and needed a nose and lip job. Yeah, that's right a nose job, and reset my jaw while I'm at it. Like a knife through butter, my self-talk ran free and without resistance it had no counter and there was no hope in sight. I didn't think I was worthy of having a relationship…even at that age. I didn't even like myself so how could I expect someone else to like me?

## Back-up arrives just in the nick of time!

One day, in my room, I don't know why but I found another voice, a supportive voice, like the feeling of pulling a warm blanket over you on a cold winter's night. It was reassuring, spoke warmly, and spoke directly to me: 'Look after your skin.' This was hope! More and more I listened to this voice, and the more I listened to it the less I heard the other. It was like déjà vu, repeating at regular intervals. You reach a fork in the road and you need to choose which road you will follow; the one that holds you in love and takes you forward to your dreams, or the one that holds you in fear, which can paralyse, and takes you back.

Please refer to the Reflection and Action section should you wish to uncover deeper insights.

## KEY 1: REFLECTION AND ACTION

### How to find your dream or purpose

Take time out to reflect. This is an exercise to do by

yourself. For me I have always loved having baths – I can stay in a bath for hours. I might zone out and switch off the lights (or add candles and music). For others it may well be spending time in nature, sitting on a beach, in a field or on top of a mountain. This is personal, it is about you. Enjoy it! See my suggestions below.

## 1. Seems so simple, but you just need to ask yourself!

Whatever is in my mind before I go to bed ends up appearing in a dream or vision as I sleep. This is the reason why I do the five things I am most grateful for today just before going to sleep. Writing down these five things in a gratitude journal, or at the very least closing your eyes and seeing those five things you were grateful for today, is a very powerful process which I highly recommend. When you're in a state of gratitude or appreciation, manifesting dreams and overcoming speedbumps comes so much more easily. In short, when you're in a good mood you're more easily able to deal with challenges than when you're in a bad mood or negative mind frame.

After your five gratitudes for the day, just before you go to sleep ask yourself out loud or in your head, what is my dream? What lights me up? What inspires me? Keep at it and monitor what happens during the next day. Repeat for a week. The key here is to stay alert during the day for coincidences or synchronicities which come your way. It could be an email, a chance meeting with a friend, phone call out of the blue, business opportunity, or something you see in a newspaper or on a billboard – just be in a state of awareness.

## 2. How to find your purpose – once again all you need to do is ask yourself!

Repeat the process above.

## 3. Meditation

Just before sleep, find somewhere quiet (or where you can hear the sounds of nature).

- Sit on the floor, bed or chair in a comfortable position with your back straight.
- Close your eyes.
- Inhale slowly in through your nose (or mouth, whichever is most comfortable).
- Focus on your breath coming down into your lungs and then follow the breath out.
- Slowly exhale (through your mouth or nose, whichever is most comfortable).
- As your mind may start wandering, just keep bringing awareness back to your breath.
- Repeat the above for five to ten minutes.
- Before going to sleep ask yourself the questions in point 1 above.

As above, be on the lookout for coincidences and synchronicities.

## 4. Ask other people

As you can see from the above I am a huge fan of allowing your own intelligence to work things out for you. I sincerely believe everything we need to succeed or achieve we have already within us. However, if you're stuck and not getting any success from the above, if you have a good friend, or someone who knows you well that you can trust, ask them. See what comes up; you're just looking to shift the initial block you may be having. Once you do, the ideas will come flooding in.

## Further support

I have found it helpful to work with meditation practitioners and have also found the teachings of Michael Domeyko Rowland (michaeldomeykorowland.com) and Shanti Mandir (shantimandir.com) beneficial.

The truth will set
you free!

# GET REAL AND ACCEPT WHAT IS, WHETHER YOU LIKE IT OR NOT!

Your thoughts,
Create your words – your words
Create your behaviour – your behaviour
Creates your habits – your habits
Create your values – and your values
Create your destiny (or results)
*Mahatma Gandhi*

### Getting real

Getting real was always a struggle for me. Do you remember what I wrote in the preface? The 'looking good' disease which has landed me in so much trouble! I heard something on television from Michael Domeyko Rowland many years ago – you know when you hear those moments of truth from an outside source that you can't ignore, as much as you want to? 'The outside world is a result of the thoughts and feelings you hold in your inner world,' he said. And it hit me hard! I think at that time I was blaming the outside world, or other people, for everything that wasn't working in my life, instead of taking responsibility.

## Repeating patterns

Do you find yourself repeating the same mistakes, for example, meeting the same kind of partner in your love life, which always ends badly? As I've told you, I'm an introverted extrovert with self-esteem challenges. So when it came down to choosing women or potential mates I would find out which people were interested in me first to cut down on the possibility of being rejected. Years ago I recall hearing this from T Harv Eker: if you want to see which repeating patterns or disempowering beliefs you have, just look at your life, that is, your results.

## Key 2 and my relationship dream

As mentioned, for a long time I found the same type of partner; actually it was the same over a twenty-five year period. I would meet an amazing girl who was attracted to me. I would think she was sexy, beautiful or attractive. We would get together and a relationship would form. We would get deep very quickly and seem to have so much in common. This honeymoon period would last for anywhere between three months to a year or more. Actually the older I got the shorter this period became. As we would continue to become closer and closer I would become scared, or start freaking out in some minor way at first, which would then increase. Then the self-talk kicked in: 'Ahh, she's not for you Rob.' Then came more pressure, ups and downs where, when I was in the moment it would be beautiful but when

I was thinking about the moment the voice would come up and remind me, 'She's not the one.'

Running parallel to this, all the things I really liked about her in the beginning, for instance, the way she played with her hair, now began to slowly annoy me – which is called 'fault finding'.

From here the pattern would repeat, becoming worse, especially the fault finding. Is this ringing any bells for you yet? This period of honeymoon, then fault finding can happen very quickly or very slowly. One of my relationships lasted for a year, the longest for over seventeen years, but the process was the same. I had three relationships in a row over twenty-five years that followed the same pattern.

## Put us out of our misery please

This fault finding is a truly nasty way for a relationship to turn; we both became petty, small-minded and toxic… quickly! Most of the time I said nothing, as in my mind I didn't want to hurt her. But when she asked me what was wrong and I didn't really say what was on my mind, it just made things worse. Around this time would be when my relationship was beginning to end. My partner, realising something wasn't gelling, would ask me what's wrong, ultimately, do we need a break? By this time I was already out the door mentally, and later physically!

This wasn't an evolved or mature way to deal with this at all. I look back and part of me cringes. There are fundamentals which give any relationship a good chance of working such as attraction, some interests in common, communication, ability to support each other, joint goals, ability to work together, whether that's physically working or working through issues which may come up. What I'm saying is that I wasn't proud of how I dealt with it. But in my last relationship I made the decision that enough was enough.

## The joys of attachment disorder

Fundamentally, my seventeen-year relationship may well have been one that wouldn't last, but in order to try and fix it, we needed to gain a deeper insight into why it wasn't working.

Landmark Forum* reminded me about my personal responsibility, which I wasn't practising at a finite level; I had an insight on fault finding, which I covered earlier on. Fault finding had nothing to do with her...it was me! Actually, the one common denominator in all those relationships was me; 'It's not you, it's me', probably the most widely used line to get out of a relationship is true, at least in this case! At that time we went to see a relationship counsellor called Akash. The most important piece of information I gleaned was the following (paraphrased) which immediately gave us perspective.

* The Landmark Forum, is a self-development conversation course. The rest, I've transcribed here from www. landmarkworlwide.com/the-landmark-forum. The Landmark Forum is designed to bring about positive, permanent shifts in the quality of your life – in just three days. These shifts

are the direct cause for a new and unique kind of freedom and power – the freedom to be at ease and the power to be effective in the areas that matter most to you: the quality of your relationships, the confidence with which you live your life, your personal productivity, your experience of the difference you make, your enjoyment of life.

## Three stages of relationships: attraction, mud and unconditional love

*Attraction:* We all know and experience this one. In the beginning everything is new, glorious and exciting. All those things he or she does you find so cute, interesting, perhaps even sexy. This honeymoon period can last for weeks, months or years – it also depends upon how often you spend quality time together.

*Mud:* It's when all your unexpressed or dormant crap comes to the surface and you project this on to your partner, and of course try to fix them! Remember the Gandhi quote at the start of this chapter? Here it is again:

> Your thoughts,
> Create your words – your words
> Create your behaviour – your behaviour
> Creates your habits – your habits
> Create your values – and your values
> Create your destiny (or results)

How you were brought up, your parents, their relationship, what you saw and experienced and the ideas and concepts placed inside your head in those early years all shape the person you have become, including the thoughts, ideas and concepts you have. In the attraction phase these rarely get touched upon. But in the mud phase they affect everything.

*Unconditional love* – this is the beautiful stage when you and your partner love, honour, accept and support each other without the need or desire to change or fix each other.

With my last relationship I was stuck in 'mud'. Only later could I give it a name – 'attachment disorder'.

'Attachment disorder' is defined as the condition in which individuals have difficulty forming lasting relationships. They often show nearly a complete lack of ability to be genuinely affectionate with others. They typically fail to develop a conscience and do not learn to trust. They do not allow people to be in control of them due to this trust issue. This damage is done by being abused, or physically or emotionally *separated from one primary caregiver during the first three years of life.* 'If a child is not attached – does not form a *loving bond with the mother* – he does not develop an attachment to the rest of mankind.' (K Magid & CA McKelvey (1988), *High risk: Children without conscience*, Bantam Books, New York).

Knowledge is power! Now I could actually do something about it. It wasn't about hiding it was about knowing what was holding me back. For example, fault finding was my way to disconnect from my partner. It was a symptom not the cause!

## Key 2 and my sport dream

As hard as I trained, as much discipline and resilience as I could muster, deep down I knew there were areas of my game that weren't improving enough. I needed to take stock, a hard look at where I was. Have you heard of a SWOT analysis? It's a diagram or an exercise that helps you to understand your Strengths, Weaknesses, Opportunities and Threats (SWOT). I'll give you an example:

**Dream – to play basketball for England under 15s**

**Strengths**

6 feet 3 and agile – ability to play in four positions

Long arms/big hands, great ability for defence against smaller, quicker players and larger slower, players

Physically strong – not easily pushed around

Great passer of the ball

Great court awareness and intuition for the game

**Weaknesses**

Concentration can sometimes wane

Not a confident shooter

Lack of foot speed when marking very quick players

**Opportunities**

Basketball clinics focusing on his weaknesses

Upcoming trial for the England squad

Ability to learn and grow

Time to develop – (currently only fifteen)

Time to mature

**Threats**

Stiff competition – there are three or four other players who can play the same position

Other players in the trial have had more time playing together

There are more experienced players out there who have been coached to a higher standard

**SWOT analysis questions**

Do any of my strengths open any opportunities?

How can I convert weaknesses into strengths?

What do I have to do to use opportunities?

How do I best neutralise threats?


You can see from the questions above the power of a SWOT type analysis and you will see the importance in the next chapter of the SWOT analysis questions. You can do it for a business but also for your own personal projects. Remember, I tripped upon this. I was so blindly committed to do whatever it took that I was in zone for a long period of time. Have you ever had the feeling, after doing something often, that you know what is coming next without even thinking about it? That's what it feels like to be in zone. In basketball, like so many other sports, it's about creating as many clear-cut opportunities to score as you can. The team that is able to convert a higher percentage of these opportunities into points will win the game.

Playing basketball for East London Royals basketball team, the players got to know each other so well on both offence and defence. For example on offence, we would know where we like the ball to be passed to us, either slightly in front of us, or to our left or right hand.

We knew where each would be on the court without even having to look. We would know which side of the opposition's defender our teammate would run to get in the best position to score. There were moments too numerous to mention when I don't even remember how we scored. Moments too numerous to mention it was like time slowed down and we would make that particular score or offensive play in slow motion, where you would see every detail, every pass and nuance which resulted in a score. Both of these are an example of being in zone as a team – and it's what you search for every game, as often as you can!

## The hope of meditation

Meditation is a master key. It took many years before I would understand what was happening and how it happened. Now I have heard so many incorrect things said about meditation that it frustrates me. I have studied with more than five meditation masters in my life, two of whom were said to be 'enlightened'. Classical Indian meditation is what I choose to follow, but whichever meditation you already follow or may decide to follow after hearing what I'm about to say, it is most likely based upon the same understanding. To meditate, translated simply means 'to focus upon', or 'draw your awareness towards'. So many times I hear 'I can't stop my thoughts' (nor can I), 'I can't get in a lotus position' (nor can I), 'I can't levitate' (nor can I) therefore I can't meditate.

Out of the five teachers, the two I connected most strongly with were more than twenty years ago, with Michael Domeyko Rowland and then his teacher Swami Nityananda from India, founder of Shanti Mandir, who was effectively handed the reins by Baba Muktananda before he passed some thirty-plus years ago. You will get to practise later on, but for now I want to get some theory into you so you realise how simple it is.

To meditate is to focus upon; I learnt firstly to focus on breath, then mantra (words). For this example we will stick to breath. I find somewhere quiet (or where I can hear the sounds of nature). I sit on the floor, bed or chair in a comfortable position with my back straight and I close my eyes. As I inhale slowly in through my nose (or mouth, whichever is most comfortable) I focus on my breath coming down into my lungs and then follow the breath out as I slowly exhale (through my mouth or through my nose, whichever is most comfortable). As my brain will invariably start wandering to all manner of things – the shopping, the washing, the conversation I was supposed to have with so and so, blah blah blah – I just keep bringing awareness back to my breath. Usually it is a case of, oh that's right I'm supposed to be meditating, and I refocus on my breath. And...that's it!

What was all the fuss about? Seriously! So simple yet people make it sound so complex; I follow my breath slowly in and out of my body maintaining my attention on my breath. When, or if, my mind wanders I bring it back to my breath again. I started meditating for five minutes, then ten minutes, then twenty, and average thirty minutes now. With regular practice the advantages are too numerous to mention, but here are a few: reduces stress, alleviates anxiety, improves concentration and brings clarity, increases happiness, increases acceptance, intuition, a deeper understanding of our inner self and our life's purpose.

You can probably see a few reasons why I'm a massive fan of meditation, and I have experienced all of the above and continue to experience it as I practise mornings, and ideally evenings too. Over the years I have used meditation in different ways, for example, I meditate about work, I meditate about my dreams and goals, my life purpose, on important decisions I must make. Meditation is to 'focus upon' so I use it to focus upon whatever is important to me at that time. Not only do I receive the health benefits, reduction in stress and anxiety and feel happier, I can better understand myself too. As I said in the beginning of the book, it's the message I connect with not so much the messenger, as human beings are fallible. There are times where I haven't practised meditation and made some awful decisions, actions and so on. But when I'm practising the results are always positive and take me in the direction of what I want to achieve.

I will keep coming back to the different ways I use meditation in the upcoming chapters so please try to complete the reflection and action section as we go.

## KEY 2: REFLECTION AND ACTION

Once again, take time out to reflect. This is an exercise you can do by yourself. For me, I have always loved having baths – I can stay in a bath for hours, I can zone out switch off the lights (or add candles and music). For others it may well be spending time in nature, sitting on a beach, in a field, or on top of a mountain. This is personal, it is about you. And once again meditation features very highly – in this case it's a way of rebooting your system. It brings you profoundly into the present moment. Here are some of my suggestions.

### 1. Meditation

This can be during the day, or at night just before sleep. Find somewhere quiet (or where you can hear the sounds of nature). **See page [184]** for a more detailed description. After following the steps above do the following:

- Find a white sheet of A4 paper (or A3).
- Write down your dream at the top.
- Underneath write 'Get Real'.
- Now write down as honestly and authentically as you can where you truly currently stand. Remember this is not where you're going to stay for much longer, but to get to where you are going you need to know where you are now. There is no set length of time or number of points you should write. The aim here is to uncover what is happening, for you to let the truth out.

- Some of you may prefer to do a SWOT analysis of the area that you have chosen.

## 2. Ask other people

As with the first key, if you're stuck and not getting any success from the above, if you have a good friend, or someone who knows you well that you can trust, ask them. See what comes up; you're just looking to shift the initial block you may be having. Once you do the ideas will come flooding in.

## Further Support

Dr John Demartini – free value-determination exercise (drdemartini.com)

Michael Domeyko Rowland (michaeldomeykorowland.com)

T Harv Eker (harveker.com)

The Landmark Forum (landmarkworldwide.com)

Jerome Lamarque (getperforming.com)

Don't quit your
day dream.

# VISUALISE, VISUALISE, VISUALISE TO THE POINT OF INSANITY!

This part of the process is by far my favourite and if you can master this then you'll be flying, but there are some pretty way-out concepts I'll go through here which may upset a few. I'd like to reinforce an important point: all I can do is write and stay true to what I do, without justifying, selling, manipulating or otherwise. The five keys work and always give me a consistent result – when I focus on them properly. I have also spent time learning why it works (some of which I share here) but I don't want to get sidetracked from the story and perhaps that can be told at a later time, in another book.

Sitting in a Michael Rowland seminar with hundreds of other people hearing that your brain can't tell the difference between what is real and what is imagined blew me away! Apparently the same neurons fire in exactly the same way when you visualise something as when it actually happens to you in real life. In all the stories I have shared so far, from sporting triumphs and bungy jumping to modelling with the supermodels, one thing I have done consistently is to visualise myself doing, it as though I'm there right now! Have you ever daydreamed? I'd say we all have. Visualising is like daydreaming to me.

One of the reflection and action steps after this chapter will be to dream a day in your life (your Lifewrite), to write it down in every detail. We take the main points and visualise them as if it is happening now. Here's an example – the car that I always wanted, a black BMW X5. I would visualise walking out of my house in the morning, seeing the black X5 parked in the driveway, feel proud of my achievement in my core, internally I let out a little 'Yeah baby – you did it!' I notice how the door handle feels and the weight of the door as I get in and close it behind me. I reach down and adjust the seat to preset number one and I feel the side lumbar supports squeeze me gently, like a warm hug from my girl. I'm in, ready to drive. Keyless entry and ignition, I put my foot on brake and push the ignition button – the engine fires up with a roar! I can smell the new car smell, I can feel the steering wheel in my hands, its leather, smooth and oversized. I check the mirror and take off, no engine lag just power, and I can see in the heads up display my speed, I take my foot off the gas. I look in the rear-vision mirror and see my friend's yellow Mini Cooper.

Now I can take it one step further. I still visualise the above except now I can overhear the conversation that I have with my partner whilst driving the car. All I need is one empowering sentence like 'I told you we'd be driving our own X5 in no time.' I visualise the happy expression and the knowing nod of approval on her face – she is proud of me and so am I.

Even though I haven't really explained it as well as I could, you can still get the feeling of what I'm trying to convey. The 'gold' is right there – it's the *feeling* of obtaining social proof which is extremely powerful, for example, 'the knowing nod'. I 'visualise the happy, expression and the knowing nod of approval on her face – she is proud of me and so am I.' How does that make you 'feel'?

I chose the car as an example, as I feel we can relate. Probably all of us drive, have driven, or have been driven in a car. When you combine this with the RAS it all just clicks into place.

## The RAS

Being in the room with Tony Robbins moved me! Actually it blew my mind! He is a globally accomplished author, teacher and self-development coach who has sold millions of books and positively affected millions more. He asked if we knew what the 'RAS' was or what it does and I didn't know what it was or what he was talking about. I'm not sure if any of the other hundreds of people in the room knew either. Apparently it refers to a small part of your brain which has a very important role; it's the gatekeeper of information that is allowed into our conscious mind. It is responsible for filtering all of the sensory data (millions of images we see every day) that we absorb and it selects the ones which are most important for our conscious mind to pay attention to. Furthermore, repeatedly visualising and holding in our mind the images or daydreams we like to create is the same as giving the RAS a direct instruction to filter that.

## Black BMW X5

I was looking for a black X5. But I hadn't seen many on the road in general. Of the ones I saw they were usually white or blue. But when I mentally, emotionally committed to researching and finding a black X5 I was sending a message to my RAS to effectively find it for me. Quite quickly and all of sudden I started seeing black X5's everywhere. Has this ever happened to you? You start looking for something which you never really noticed before then all of a sudden you start seeing it everywhere!

## Bringing it together

When I combined the power of visualisation and the awareness of the RAS and what it does, my life took a massive turn! Anything I have achieved so far has hinged on the use of dream building, Lifewrite, visualisation and the RAS; they work together and earlier I mentioned meditation as a supercharger!

## Synchronicity

I don't know how an internal combustion engine works, all I know is when I insert the key, start the engine, take my foot off the brake (if an automatic) and put it in gear the cars moves forwards! Just like when I spoke about basketball, the aim is to create as many scoring opportunities as possible and the team which does this and converts these opportunities at a higher percentage wins. It's the same in life! It's about creating opportunities to succeed but you still have to take ACTION!

All the above is doing is creating synchronicity or opportunities to succeed. Synchronicity is like a lucky coincidence. Those of you reading this who are in a relationship, think about how you met your partner. Then think about how many other opportunities there were. I met my partner Marina at friend's barbecue. I hadn't seen that friend for a long time, and I wasn't supposed to even attend; I had three other engagements that night and at the last minute I decided to 'drop in' to that one and ended up staying and not going to the others. Lucky coincidence? You can see a pattern throughout my story of being in the right place at the right time! Lucky! Franco the photographer in Milan and the back door into Ricardo Gay modelling agency, working for the Madonna MTV Music Awards in Milan, meeting, talking to and hanging out with Samuel L Jackson, Lawrence Fishburne, Ian Thorpe, INXS the list is long. Time and time and time again. Can someone really be that lucky? Can I really be that lucky? Like I said, I don't know how a car works…but it does. I don't know how this works in every detail but it does, and has done for more than twenty years of using it, even though at first it was not consciously.

**How to supercharge your way to success**

I combine meditation with this process. After entering a state of meditation for fifteen to twenty minutes, I feel calm, I feel centred, I feel in tune with my body, and at this stage I purposefully plant my visualisation. I imagine deeply. I think of the supportive conversations I have with willing participants, I see the look in their eye – they are proud me. I see me driving the car, smelling the car, feeling the surge of power beneath my feet, the rush of adrenaline and excitement coursing through my veins I can see myself in the picture like a movie playing over and over again in which I have the leading role.

I repeat this process every morning and every evening and as many times during each day as I can remember to do so – if I'm travelling by train, taxi or as a passenger in a car.

## Taking action

This step is vital. So often I sit and see opportunities rolling past out of fear! I feel like I'm clamming up, no longer fearless when I make decisions. Synchronicity takes you so far, it creates the opportunity, like bringing a horse to water – but you can't make it drink. The horse needs to decide. Imagine me at the barbecue seeing Marina but not talking to her, actually ignoring her completely!

## Key 3 and my sport dream

As you know from my description earlier, I worked really hard for my dream of playing basketball for England. I went to basketball clinics up and down the country to learn new skills which would help me, I learned how to run faster, I learned how to shoot more accurately, I stayed behind after school to practise, as well as lunchtimes, sometimes even before school started I would be shooting in the gym. When other kids were playing in the playground, I would be inside doing shooting drills. I researched the best team in the area to get into, East London Royals, I trialled and was accepted. I worked harder than anyone else because I wasn't the best player. I felt athletic, I felt agile and nimble like a jaguar with really long arms and legs. I kept practising. It became an obsession. I would think about it, dream about it. I'd watch it on TV and I'd go watch games. My coach Humph put me forward for the South-East England team. I trialled and managed to get in. I was consumed, I was focused and I was ready but still not confident in my abilities – so I worked harder to compensate.

All the above looks like a lot of activity going on – training, learning how to run faster and shoot more accurately. I was busy, but what if I told you that I spent just as much time, if not more, visualising my outcome; more importantly, tapping into the feelings. Especially, how would I feel if? How would I feel if I was playing basketball for England, that is, if I was playing basketball for England how would I feel when I ran out on court to warm up with the other players? How would I feel listening to the crowd shouting and screaming? What feelings would I have in the game when I scored? How would I feel after I scored, looking up at the electronic scoreboard seeing the points next to my name? I created my Lifewrite script around it. This led to synchronicities all over the place, to mention a few, finding the East London Royals in the first place in time for the trials, the coach having a say/input into the selection of the England squad and finding teammates who were from the same background as me.

## Key 3 and my relationship dream

I was coming out of a seventeen-year relationship and had been doing some work with a great coach, Jerome Lamarque. The work we were doing was all about getting clear what kind of partner I was looking for, but prior to that, what I was looking for myself? What were my values, what was I interested in doing, what I wanted my life to look like, feel like and be like. I was tapping into my feelings already as I had come to the realisation that my current relationship had run its course. We had tried to rescue it and save it but fundamentally we were not going to reach the next stage. So I was already visualising what it would feel like to find a partner that I would be able to move forward with, who I could support and inspire, as they could do for me in turn, and who I could have a family with. I visualised a life with children, I visualised a life with a family of my own. I was dialled in. I knew what I wanted in my next and hopefully last life partner.

I hope you're getting the hang or concept of visualising – it really is like daydreaming and we have all done that before…so you can do this!

Please complete the reflection and action section of this chapter…the last two keys are just a few pages away.

## KEY 3: REFLECTION AND ACTION

Once again, take time out to reflect. This is an exercise you can do by yourself. That's right! Reboot first by meditating, having a bath, or being in nature, listening to your favourite music – whichever gets you in the zone and profoundly into the present moment!

### 1. Meditation

This can be during the day, or at night just before sleep. Find somewhere quiet (or where you can hear the sounds of nature). **See page [184]** for a more detailed description.

### 2. Lifewrite

This is based upon the work of Michael Domeyko Rowland.

- Find a white sheet of A3 paper or even larger.
- Write down the dream you're working towards at the top.
- Underneath, write 'Visualise'.
- Divide your life up into five areas: Career, Health, Business, Relationships and Personal Growth. Under which section or area could you add the dream you are currently working on?
- Under each area write down all of your most important dreams over the next one to two years, at least three under each heading – this may take a few hours. Even though we are focusing on one you can also see how it fits into the whole picture. As an aside, you may even start to think how you could achieve each one. You may need to study, head

back to university or get back into training to fulfil a sporting dream. I'm not asking you for precisely how you are going to do it, but to start considering.

- Once you have your areas mapped out you can start to add them to your Lifewrite.
- Let's start with a one-year Lifewrite, for example. Life writing is a way to write down your dream in the future as if you are living it, or writing it into the present moment, or as if it has already happened. Let me give you an example from the Lifewrite I wrote in 2016:
- It is January 2017 and I am extremely inspired and wake up with a positive state of mind EVERY DAY!
- Marina and I are having fun building and growing our businesses whilst spending plenty of quality time together as a family including driving trips in the family car – my Black BMW X5M. All of our kids are doing really well; they're secure in themselves, independent, very happy, have their own personalities and know we love them dearly. We're comfortable and happy focusing on our future together: living in Bali for 2–3 months of the year and Sydney for the remainder.

You can see from here that there are a few dreams interwoven into it. As it stands, at the moment of writing this, our family have been in Bali for six months already. Our kids are as described and we have been having fun building our cafe/fashion businesses and are set to build another in Bali.

This a brief excerpt from my larger Lifewrite, which filled up just over an A4 sheet – I read it religiously day and night, on waking up and before going to bed. To add more power I would add visualisation into it. I would find a key section of my Lifewrite such as this:

> Each week my work in the community for the community is growing which further enamours us to our customers, clients and locals alike. I love doing it and it fulfils my life purpose and is a point of difference and strength to many other café businesses in Redfern, whilst, in the case of CSWP boxing program, keeps me physically fit too. It's a win-win for everyone!

For example, with the above I would visualise in great detail my time boxing with the kids and the interaction with the mentors of the program; visualise and feel my contentment in my skin so vividly it was as though I was there. Remember the brain doesn't know the difference between what is imagined and what is 'real' the same neurons fire the same hormones secreted into the body. Go back to the chapter in the book to see my example.

Find a key section or area of your Lifewrite that you would like to work on and create a mini-movie visualisation of between one and three minutes. You could include some dialogue too.

At any time of the day or night, whenever you have a few minutes, you can tap in and play your movie. Each week you can change up and choose a different part of your Lifewrite to create a movie.

## Further support

Michael Domeyko Rowland – Absolute Happiness (michaeldomeykorowland.com)

Natalie Ledwell – Mind Movies (mindmovies.com)

In order to make dreams a reality, it takes an awful lot of determination, dedication, self-discipline and effort.

– Jesse Owens

# ANNIHILATING THOSE SELF-SABOTAGE PATTERNS (SPEED BUMPS)

Speed bumps.

So many times it felt like I could achieve the goal I'd set for myself only to fall short at the last minute. I was becoming a 'nearly guy', a person who had all the talent and ability in the world to overcome obstacles, but didn't make it. It reminded me of bungy jumping in Taupo, New Zealand in the early 1990s.

Your WHY is what provides you the willpower, the sticking power to go through all of the steps and finally achieve the dream. It is the starting point and masterkey to obtaining resilience. It's the reason, when it feels like the world is beating you down, you keep getting back up. All the racism, the beatings, the fights, don't get me started on the 'class structure' divide, the unfairness of what happened to some of my fellow orphans – it primed me, it gave me permission to be dogged, determined, to never give up, as I was fighting for something far larger and more important than myself! We all have a dream inside of us, no matter how large or small, but it takes courage, sacrifice and often getting uncomfortable and reaching outside of ourselves to achieve it. Sometimes you need to move house or move country to obtain it. Sometimes you may need to leave unsupportive friendships that act as an anchor, keeping you stuck to the seabed when you need to get going! But if you commit to the process, all of the above will happen without you thinking about it.

## Key 4 and my sport dream

The England trials came up at a training camp and I felt out of my depth. I wasn't confident in my offensive abilities but where I did feel comfortable was my ability to defend, to snatch the ball away from my opposite marker utilising my unfeasibly long telescopic arms. I'd pluck the ball out of passing lanes. I'd anticipate where the ball was going and steal it. I had the athleticism to mark players taller than me or shorter and quicker than me. I found my spot! If I was playing American Football I'd be a defensive specialist. I worked so hard that I surprised myself. I went from a person of little focus and discipline to a person consumed with 'drive' and passion – I was in it to win it. I woke up inspired by it and I went to bed dreaming about it. Was I to be the first person from a children's home to make it into the England under-15 basketball team?

## Reaching out for purpose

Living in the children's homes as I did and especially 3 The Ridgeway, exposed me to the best and worst things I have ever experienced in my life. To watch Andy Campbell taking a kicking for me during that racist attack in South Chingford made me sick to my stomach, embarrassed, confused and filled with hate! I used sport, like rugby, on the trip up north to really vent my anger and aggression on the world. I was mad, upset, confused and pissed off and I wanted to make someone pay. But deep down I knew it was me, it was always me who let myself down. Why wasn't I able to stick up for myself? Why wasn't I able to fight back instead of feeling paralysed? Why did people treat me differently because of my skin colour? Why did the mods attack our house? Why did the police not stick up for us instead of trying to arrest us? Probably the most defining question of all, why did I want to be white instead of black growing up? However, no matter how hard I tried, it just wasn't in me to fight and get in the kind of trouble that would land me in jail. It was like a guiding hand from above kept steering me away from getting in serious trouble. Perhaps I was just too scared! I'd seen what happened to Lee (you remember his story back in the initial chapters).

### Key 4 and my relationship dream

In the beginning Marina and I had our differences; it was clear that we had similarities but we were also different people. It took us time to build up a trust and respect for one another. I have so much respect for her, especially through the two pregnancies. It's an all-consuming episode that continues for many months, and it is not easy. Our relationship was fresh we had a business that we'd only just built, with all the demands of a modern-day life in Sydney and with no support from parents or relatives. But we had a focus. She to me was the embodiment of a woman I was very happy and proud to be with. Fundamentally we gelled as well. I reminded myself of the three stages of relationships, which Akash taught. I wanted to start this relationship well and there were still times that I felt out of my depth. But all the training, understanding and learning from past relationships, driven by the desire to also sire a family with Marina, came to be very beneficial for the both of us.

## The bungy solution to speed bumps!

Back in New Zealand in the 1990s, Nics my-ex and I had decided to bungy jump. Before we did we decided to look from a distance to see just what we were getting ourselves into it. We sat on a grassy knoll watching the bungy jumpers leap from the manmade platform which protruded over the edge of a steep-sided river valley and 80 to 100 metres below was the river itself. We watched in cross-section about 100 metres away. As they jumped and screamed off the platform, down and down into the water below, some went all the way in, hands, arms and head first, whilst others submerged their whole torso.

It was a beautiful blue sky, clear afternoon in New Zealand but the air had a cool bite to it, like a frosty breeze down your neck when you forget to zip your jacket all the way up on a freezing cold morning! I was scared of bungy jumping but excited by it at the same time. Some of the jumpers were so elegant, soaring like eagles until the cable sucked them back up – a spectacular sight. I thought, 'I want to be like them.' But what really caught my eye wasn't the successes but the failures!

We were there watching when a lady came on to the platform, with the harness strapped around her feet. She shuffled out to the platform as one of the tech guys ran through the final checks and explained the sequence of events. Her hands clasped the two parallel bars on either side of the narrow gap you jump out of. She looked look down into the river below and immediately lost all courage to jump, like water draining out of the kitchen sink as soon as the plug is removed. Three-two-one bungeeeee! Instead of her hands releasing the parallel bars and jumping forwards, outwards and downwards in a perfectly executed swallow dive, she was paralysed! Unable to move. Unable to take her hands off the rail. They shook uncontrollably and her body shut down and went into 'freeze mode'. She regained herself and said she was okay. Three-two-one bungeeeee! This happened four or five times I counted. Until finally she jumped. Not really a jump. Nor a dive. It was like watching a picture peel off the wall and fall down to the floor; it happened in slow motion, as if the Blu Tack wasn't strong enough to hold it. I'd never seen anything like it. Her scream seemed to last twice as long as anyone else we'd seen that hour. Even her freefall seemed twice as long as anyone else. Honestly, it put us off doing it!

Looking back though, I wonder what kind of

determination that lady had to keep going back. Not to give up. Actually instead of ridiculing that lady, I soon was in awe of her resilience – admittedly at first I did have a giggle (sorry).

For the record, we did jump that day. I'm laughing as I'm writing this because of what comes next. I got to the same position – bungy connected, shuffle out to the edge, don't look down, which of course I did. In this moment I realised doing bungy must be like committing suicide! Every nerve, fibre, muscle, brain cell in my body tells me to stop! I don't see the bungy cord attached to my ankles. I don't even see my legs. As I look straight ahead then down I see sky, trees, grass, cliffs, rocks, river and a tiny narrow open gate to jump through. It's madness! Countdown begins: three – I feel my body freezing up, two – fuck it! I Jump! The best swallow dive I could muster. I see trees, grass, cliffs, ground rush. I pick up tremendous speed, the cliffs are rushing by me. The sound in my ears is an intensely loud feedback from a stereo. I struggle to push my arms out and maintain my form. I'm not breathing. My vision is narrowing. I become aware of this high-pitched noise outside of the feedback. It's me screaming! The water is approaching really fast and I have no way of stopping. Is this it? Is this how I die? I hope that bungy cord kicks in any moment…suddenly I feel a sharp pull. My guts feel like they're shoved into my mouth. For a second – am I going to vomit? Oh no, not now! Tenths of seconds pass. This feeling is replaced by elation. It's like an orgasm.

## The 'why' exercise

There are many forms of this exercise but I like to stick to the simplest – writing down 300 reasons why you want that dream so much! It sounds like a huge number at first but once you start this opinion will change. You may feel as though you are going round and round in circles or repeating yourself. This is just your mind throwing up excuses – just keep on ploughing through. Like panning for gold you will hit quite a few nuggets, those reasons why which are so compelling to you that your realise that you can't, won't and refuse to be stopped. I have left another two or three different modalities in the reflection and action section of this chapter on how to overcome roadblocks – meditation, 70 x 7 and EFT tapping.

You are almost there now, just complete one of the tools for overcoming speed bumps in the reflection and action section then come back to finish off the fifth and final key. The good news, there's no reflection and action section for the final key!

## KEY 4: REFLECTION AND ACTION

Reboot and reconnect to yourself by meditating first. By now you may be feeling the vibe of meditating and start a semi-regular or regular practice. Now we going to see another great use meditation can offer. Remember, to meditate means 'to focus upon or reflect upon'. The process of focusing upon can also be used to help us gain clarity on our sabotage patterns or speed bumps. I have used the process of meditation to reflect on problems and challenges in order to find solutions. Here are some of my suggestions.

## 1. Meditation

This can be during the day, or at night just before sleep. Find somewhere quiet (or where you can hear the sounds of nature). **See page [184]** for a more detailed description.

- When you feel your mind has stabilised, i.e. you feel calm with not too many thoughts running around your head, see your challenge and ask for the solution.

- Maintain your breathing, except now you are reflecting on your challenge or roadblock and getting clear on what it is. Often you may find the solutions start to present themselves. Repeat this process for as long as needed i.e. until you reach a resolution.

- You may also repeat the process above, then before going to sleep ask yourself what you would like to get clear on i.e. the solution.

- As per before, be on the lookout the next day/s for guidance via coincidences and synchronicities.

## 2. The 'why' exercise

As mentioned earlier, there are many forms of this exercise, but the simplest is often the most powerful.

- Set aside at least an hour where you won't be disturbed.

- Reboot yourself with a short meditation of ten

minutes, then find a white sheet of A4 paper (or A3) and write down your dream at the top.

- Now write down as honestly and authentically as you can 300 or more reasons why you really want that dream or outcome!
- Free write! In other words, whatever comes into your mind, no matter what it is.
- Don't be stopped. This is just your mind throwing up excuses – just keep on ploughing through. Like panning for gold you will hit quite a few nuggets. As mentioned above, you will discover those reasons which are so compelling to you that you realise that you can't, won't and refuse to be stopped.

## 3. The 70 x 7

This is another Michael Domeyko Rowland inspired exercise I used to remove the subconscious blocks, some of which I didn't even know were there. This is another writing exercise which can take up to an hour or so a day for seven days in a row, without missing a day or any excuses.

- Find an empty, lined book or several pieces of A4 paper (preferably lined).
- Write 'No. 1' and next to it write down the dream that you're working on and put it into a succinct, positive' sentence in the present', as if you are achieving it already. For example, 'I am now playing basketball for the England under-15 basketball team.' Or to evoke more emotion, 'I am now playing

starting five for the England under-15 basketball team.' Or if relationship based, 'I am now in a loving, supportive relationship with my beautiful partner and it feels great.'

- Write down the first thing that comes into your head (no filtering) on the next line or lines (depending how long it is).
- When there is nothing left to write move to the next free line and write 'No. 2' and write out the phrase again and the response on the next line.
- Don't pay attention to what's written, just keep going, seventy times.

After you are finished there is no reason to read your results either. What's happening is that you are removing the subconscious blockers and after seven days in a row you can tear it all up, burn it, or bin it – it is up to you. I used to make it into a bit of a ceremony and burn it, but it's entirely up to you. The key is seven days in a row and not to be stopped or self-sabotage!

### 4. The tapping solution (EFT) by Nick Ortner

Tapping, also known as EFT (Emotional Freedom Techniques), is a powerful holistic healing technique that has been proven to effectively resolve a range of issues, including stress, anxiety, phobias, emotional disorders, chronic pain, addiction, weight control, and limiting beliefs, just to name a few.

Tapping therapy is based on the combined principles

of ancient Chinese acupressure and modern psychology. Tapping with the fingertips on specific meridian endpoints of the body, while focusing on negative emotions or physical sensations, helps to calm the nervous system, rewire the brain to respond in healthier ways, and restore the body's balance of energy.

In short, tapping gives you the power to heal yourself. It's not difficult to master and is easy to learn. Instead of running through the process here, it is more appropriate for you to go directly to Nick's site and introduction webinar at thetappingsolution.com/tapping-101.

## Further Support

Michael Domeyko Rowland (michaeldomeykorowland.com)
Dr John Demartini (drdemartini.com)
Nick Ortner (thetappingsolution.com)

We are at our most
powerful the moment
we no longer need to
be powerful.

– Eric Micha'el Leventhal

# SURRENDER – GIVE IT TIME, MOST GIVE UP TOO SOON!

**M**aking it this far in this book you have done me a great honour and now, as promised, I'm going to put it all together for you. Let me remind you (and me) of how far we have come. Step by step you have seen me emerge from a cocoon of sorts, like a larva becoming a butterfly. You have seen my flaws, my mistakes, some of my successes, you've seen an insatiable desire to keep learning, to keep moving forward and above all not to give up. I've conveyed these to you for two reasons: number one you have these traits too, we all do! And number two, which is the main message of this book, no matter where you're from or what your background, it is where you are going that counts. Importantly, you can have success, overcoming adversity and achieving your dreams along the way; it's just about having a roadmap to guide you there, and that is what this part of the book is all about. For the best results fill in the answers to the questions as honestly and authentically as you can – the more honest you are the deeper the transformation.

This key is probably the most frustrating of the five keys! How many times have you just given up too soon on something? Or failed to recognise the signs? Or realised 'this is just not for me' or it isn't what you thought it would be. Completion! Writing this book I'm experiencing this again too. But there is hope, and without becoming too 'out there and esoteric', there really is a divine timing to the universe. Putting this aside for now, I've noticed, depending on the level of complexity of my dreams, within three months I start to see significant movements in synchronicity and opportunity towards achieving them, whilst long-term goals can take just that…years. When I'm in the zone, I'll be meditating in the morning for twenty to thirty minutes. I'll read my Lifewrite aloud if conditions permit, otherwise silently, I'll remain alert for synchronicity towards achieving my dreams every day (I do expect miracles every day). I remain relaxed and as calm as I can in my quiet times and remember to breathe and enjoy as many moments as I can, whether that's playing with the kids and generally practising mindfulness (remaining focused on what you are doing). Before I go to sleep I write or at the very least recall five things that I'm grateful for today in my gratitude diary. I may also do a guided meditation.

## Most people give up too soon!

Years ago when I was in a self-development seminar (I can't remember which one, perhaps a Robert Kiyosaki seminar) the presenter spoke about creative tension. It made perfect sense. It's like an elastic band that you pull apart using your hands. The further you pull the stronger the resistance or the force trying to bring it back together again. Imagine one end of the elastic band is your current reality and on the other is your dream! If you can hold this tension for long enough (primarily visualising, overcoming speedbumps and maintaining a positive state of mind) your dream will meet your current reality as both ends of the elastic band spring back in towards each other! When I heard this it made me think of all the times I had failed to maintain this tension and gave up too soon. But also during this period of time I find out how much I actually want it and if that goal is even important to me at all. This is what I spoke about earlier in relation to 'heart goals' and how strong your why is. Whenever I have connected to a heart goal I have always achieved it. Or if my reasons why were profound enough, I always achieved it.

## Key 5 and my sport dream

For example, when I wanted to play basketball for England I also had injuries. I rolled my ankle the night before one of the trials. I was devastated when I felt it click when I rolled over the football I was playing with the night before. My heart jumped up into the back of my throat then sunk like a stone in the bottom of my stomach! I'd blown my shot! I wept as I saw my dreams go up in smoke right in front of my eyes. Stupid, stupid, stupid! What was I doing even playing football the night before anyway! But here's the thing, straight after this, my reason why replaced the negative mind chatter like the sun replaces the moon from night to day. The bullying and racism I'd endured, I was an ambassador, all of the children, staff and adults at 3 The Ridgeway were relying on me, it was my chance to put us all on the map. I wasn't doing this just for me I was doing it for them and black people in general. With a heavily strapped ankle and pain (I told no-one) I got through that trial the next day. I couldn't fail!

On average over the years, three months seems to be the time I have noticed significant change or progress towards achieving the goal that I set…so long as I have done the work, that is, steps one to five on a regular basis! Define the dream or goal, ascertain where you are now, visualise frequently, and overcome roadblocks and time!

## Key 5 and my relationship dream

Once again, on this occasion I was fortunate the work I had done on this brought things to fruition within three months. What did it for Marina and I was the desire to raise a family. Within a short time of being together, we both arrived in the same place of understanding; if we were going to be together and committed the time was now! As I mentioned before, the honeymoon period is diminishing more and more rapidly with each relationship and after six months we had built a business and were pregnant with our first baby.

## Divine timing

Just like the ability to see the forest through the trees, focusing on one event or outcome to the exclusion of everything else, it's the ability to look at something holistically (as a whole) instead of looking at solely at 'what's in for me'!

The first section of this book is littered with examples of 'luck' or what I call divine timing, such as walking into that small courtyard in Milan to see the photographer, Franco, when I did. Had I been moments later I would have missed him crossing the same courtyard. The way we hiked the Tongariro Crossing in New Zealand, ill-prepared, as the rapidly changing alpine conditions left us stranded and in danger, when suddenly we literally bumped into those two prepared climbers in square miles of alpine plateau which we couldn't even see as visibility was so poor – talk about finding the needle in the haystack!

I really am happy to be alive and living on planet earth and so happy that I've managed to finish my very first book. I really do hope that you have gained at least one thing from it which will help you on your journey.

A sincere thank you!

# PART 6
# A PARTING WORD

Our journey is now nearing its climax. I hope that something in this book has been of value to you, or sparked an interest to see how amazing each and every one of us can truly be. I hope that this has reminded you of what you capable of, and the fact that miracles can be part of your daily life if you expect them. The five keys outlined in this book have served me well when I have really practised them (horribly when I haven't) and meditation as a masterkey is the most valuable resource available to you, in my opinion. As mentioned before I am a lifelong learner, even after writing this book there are other hacks (or shortcuts) I've been road testing to further expedite the journey from dream to activation, but the information herein is the truth of what got me where I was at the time of writing it. But I digress.

Remember, the central premise of this book is: it's not where you start in life, it's where you are going that's important. The methodologies in some areas may be upgraded but it's down to your core drivers, which I have explained before, but some of the key ones, I believe will always apply. Identifying what your dream is and having the courage of dealing with whatever is in your way ie. why you will not be stopped until you achieve it! The ability to visualise your outcome as often as you can (each day) and acting as though it is already achieved. You must recognise the role of synchronicity – whilst taking effective action throughout, especially when the opportunities arise. Learning to remain focused and overcome any challenges. Finally, acknowledging and surrendering to the role of time. Armed with this knowledge, would you ask yourself honestly, where is my current trajectory taking me? Then you have an important choice to make! The beauty is that it is not too late to start right now from wherever you are without hesitation! To this end I leave you below a reminder and one of my favourite quotes I refer to often ...

From the bottom of my heart, thank you for reading this book to the end and sharing in my journey – I really do appreciate it. If you have picked up even one nugget or insight of what to do (even of what not to do) from what you have read, then this project has been a success and worthy of your commitment to complete!

Until next time.

RiB

"Until one is committed, there is hesitancy, the chance to draw back, always ineffectiveness. Concerning all acts of initiative and creation, there is one elementary truth the ignorance of which kills countless ideas and splendid plans: that the moment one definitely commits oneself, then providence moves too. All sorts of things occur to help one that would never otherwise have occurred. A whole stream of events issues from the decision, raising in one's favour all manner of unforeseen incidents, meetings and material assistance which no man could have dreamed would have come his way. Whatever you can do or dream you can, begin it. Boldness has genius, power and magic in it. Begin it now."

– Johann Wolfgang von Goethe

First published in 2018 by New Holland Publishers
London • Sydney • Auckland

131-151 Great Titchfield Street, London WIW 5BB, United Kingdom
1/66 Gibbes Street, Chatswood, NSW 2067, Australia
5/39 Woodside Ave, Northcote, Auckland 0627, New Zealand

newhollandpublishers.com

Copyright © 2018 New Holland Publishers
Copyright © 2018 in text: Robert Bonnick
Copyright © 2018 in images: Robert Bonnick

All rights reserved. No part of this publication may be reproduced, stored in
a retrieval system or transmitted, in any form or by any means, electronic,
mechanical, photocopying, recording or otherwise, without the prior written
permission of the publishers and copyright holders.

A record of this book is held at the British Library and the National Library
of Australia.

ISBN 9781742575957

Group Managing Director: Fiona Schultz
Publisher: Monique Butterworth
Project Editor: Liz Hardy
Designer: Catherine Meachen
Production Director: James Mills-Hicks
Printer: Toppan Leefung Printing Limited

10 9 8 7 6 5 4 3 2 1

Keep up with New Holland Publishers on Facebook
facebook.com/NewHollandPublishers